Tommy Bahama®

LIFE IS ONE LONG WEEKEND™

Tommy Bahama®

LIFE IS ONE LONG WEEKEND™

DK · Tommy Bahama®

DK

LONDON, NEW YORK, MUNICH,
MELBOURNE, DELHI

FOR DORLING KINDERSLEY

Editor CÉCILE LANDAU

Project Manager ROS WALFORD

Project Art Editor LEE RICHES

DTP Designers DAVID MCDONALD, KAVITA VARMA

Special Sales Production Manager SILVIA LA GRECA BERTACCHI

Senior Production Controller RACHEL LLOYD

Associate Publisher NIGEL DUFFIELD

Sales Manager ABE CHANG

Tommy Bahama®

FOR TOMMY BAHAMA

Chief Executive Officer TERRY PILLOW

President and COO DOUG WOOD

Creative Directors LANCE RELICKE, JOSHUA CAMPBELL

Editorial Advisor NATALIE CHERMAK

Destination photography DAVE LAURIDSEN

Color reproduction by MDP Ltd, UK.
Printed and bound in the U.S.A. by Lake Book Manufacturing, Inc.

This American Edition, 2010
First American Edition, 2010

Published in the United States by
DK Publishing, Inc.
375 Hudson Street,
New York, New York 10014

10 11 12 13 10 9 8 7 6 5 4 3 2

Published in Great Britain by Dorling Kindersley Limited.
A Cataloging-in-Publication record for this book is available from the Library of Congress.

ISBN 978-0-7566-6095-6

Discover more at
www.dk.com

contents

introduction

LIFE IS ONE LONG WEEKEND… This is the carefree philosophy of Tommy Bahama, the lifestyle brand that elevates the act of relaxation to a fine art. The Tommy Bahama concept debuted in 1992 with a collection of upscale mens' casual sportswear. Since then, the company has evolved into a complete lifestyle collection that includes womens' sportswear, swimwear, golf clothing, accessories, home furnishings, retail stores, restaurants, and rum. In 1996, Tommy Bahama opened its first store and restaurant in Naples, Florida. The company soon expanded and it now has facilities in more than 80 locations.

The inspiration behind the company is a fictional character—Tommy Bahama—who enjoys a peaceful island lifestyle. He shows you how to obtain this slow-paced, relaxed way of living—no matter where you live or what time of year. There's something magical about finding a place—even your own home—where the only requirement is to unwind. And it's so easy to bring the Tommy Bahama philosophy into your home. With the ultimate Purveyor of Island Lifestyles as your guide, entertaining family and friends takes on a new level of sophistication and you'll learn to make the most of the finer things in life.

seeking paradise

"…Relax, slow down, the island lifestyle is waiting…Escape…to a life that's one long weekend…steel drums, soft sand, palms wafting in the breeze…"

The Perfect Beach

According to legend, the first earthly paradise was Eden, a lush, verdant garden of delights, a place of peace and plenty, where life was easy, and free from stress and strife. The golden, sun-kissed beaches of the tropics still offer a taste of Eden today. Mile upon mile of soft, powdery white sand, fringed with swaying palms and dotted with secluded, rocky bays, create a paradise within your grasp.

Just how you define your perfect beach will depend on what you are seeking. A quiet, secluded bay may make the ideal backdrop for romance, or it might offer calm, crystal-clear waters in which to indulge your passion for scuba diving or sailing.

Maybe you want to play, dine, or just chill out with family and friends. Or perhaps you wish to explore the many natural wonders and curiosities of the tropical world, or are simply searching for a picturesque place to relax and watch the world go by.

So escape to the tropics, where there's a "perfect" paradise beach to match every taste and meet every desire.

"Endless, year-round sunshine, intoxicating ocean breezes, and the gentle ebb and flow of clear, azure-blue waters will bring you your own little corner of Eden..."

Escaping

Even in the midst of the hustle and bustle of daily life, you can escape to "paradise." Just thinking about your perfect tropical beach can help you to shed those stresses and strains, to experience deep relaxation, and to re-energize. Create a paradise in your own home by designing tranquil areas in which to hide away. Make time for life's pleasures and adopt a healthy lifestyle that will help you to develop a strong body and lively, inquiring mind. Harness the soothing power of your imaginary island paradise and let your worries float away.

Stress-Busting Techniques

◀ *Yoga* The steady, controlled movements, gentle stretching, and deep breathing involved in yoga can help to induce a meditative state of deep calm. In addition, yoga will give you a more flexible and toned body, which means you'll be fitter and better equipped to tackle life's challenges in a more positive way. You'll look good too, and that will boost your confidence and lift your spirits.

▶ *Meditation* Focusing fully on good feelings and thoughts is a great way to relax and achieve total peace. One approach is to close your eyes and "plant" an image in your mind of your perfect tropical paradise. Picture yourself wandering through it, then focus on, say, the back of your neck, and visualize all the muscles relaxing and the tension oozing out of them. Move to your shoulders, then to your back, and do the same. Area by area, drift down to your toes and feel all the stress that you are holding onto melt away.

▲ *Get Active* Attaining a state of deep relaxation isn't the only way to beat stress. If a little action is what gets you going, why not take up golf, play tennis, or hike through the countryside near your home to burn up all that pent-up energy and frustration? You'll certainly get fitter, which can help to banish stress—and you may even make a few new friends that will bring some extra fizz into your social life at the same time.

Stress

◀ *At Home* Bringing the tropics into your home is a great way to achieve a relaxing living space. Go for furnishings that reflect the colors and mood of the tropics—the soft white and rich gold of a sandy beach, the sparkling blue of the ocean, the deep greens and browns of the palms, and the dazzling rainbow hues of tropical flowers. Create areas for relaxation and meditation, festooned with cushions draped with exotic fabrics.

▼ *Time Out at a Spa* Sometimes it's best to just lie back and let someone else work the tension out of those stiff, tired muscles. The pampering and indulgence of a massage, especially with a blend of richly aromatic oils that are specially chosen to elevate your mood, is a heavenly way to restore well-being and vitality. Steam out some of the tension and toxins from your body first by taking a Turkish bath or sauna, then follow your massage with a relaxing hour or so around the spa pool.

◀ *Fresh Horizons* Simply imagining those soft, refreshing tropical breezes wafting over you can give you a lift, perhaps making you more open to new interests and activities. Let thoughts of your perfect beach inspire you to grab a paint brush and see if you can capture some of its magical beauty on canvas. Learn to scuba dive, so that you can explore the wonders of a tropical ocean bed or coral reef, or try sailing, so that you can venture farther to the more remote parts of "paradise."

▶ *Healthy Eating* Preparing and eating dishes with that tropical touch—delicious, freshly barbecued meats and seafood, juicy mangoes and pineapples, creamy coconuts—can transport you back mentally to your paradise island. There is also the bonus that a diet of such fragrant and fresh produce, cooked in a simple, unfussy manner, is both highly nutritious and easy to digest, providing you with the extra zest to enjoy life to the full.

paradise approaching

"*Life is an adventure…Be curious, be bold…Make the world your playground…Step out and explore the fascinating places and myriad wonders all around you…Somewhere, maybe just around the corner, there's a paradise waiting, just for you…*"

LAS VEGAS

It's certainly true that the lights shine brighter in Las Vegas than almost anywhere else. In Nevada's glitziest city, you'll find the biggest stars in show business and some of the world's most luxurious hotels, casinos, shops, and restaurants. And just outside the city are some spectacular natural attractions including glowing deserts, deep canyons, and extraordinary rock formations—as well as the colossal Hoover Dam, one of the engineering wonders of the world.

In the heart of the city is Las Vegas Boulevard, a sparkling vista of neon known as "The Strip." This 3.5-mile (6-km) street is lined with lavishly themed hotels, including Bellagio, Caesars Palace, Luxor, and the Venetian. They attract almost 37 million visitors each year, making Las Vegas the entertainment capital of the world.

KONA On Hawai'i Island's beautiful Pacific coast, the diverse district of Kona boasts superb watersports, sunsets—and coffee. The bustling town of Kailua-Kona makes a great base for exploring the region, from the pretty beaches that fleck its sunny coastline to the giant volcanoes, lava fields, and ancient sites of the island's interior. Marine pleasure-seekers will delight in spotting dolphins and whales, fishing for ocean giants, or snorkeling the island's finest natural aquarium at Kahalu'u Beach.

The fertile slopes of the Kona district are home to the United States' only coffee-growing region. The massive bulk of Mauna Loa volcano creates a sheltered environment that favors the crop here. In Kona's coffee belt, roadsides are dotted with cafés, mills, and small coffee farms, which look out across the sublime coastal landscape.

NAPLES

This wealthy beach city prides itself on its manicured beauty, championship golf courses, and pristine, sugary beaches. Naples has a laid-back charm where endless days can be spent exploring its high-end clothes shops, art galleries, and restaurants, or sailing and charter-fishing in the calm Gulfshore waters. The region also offers thrills for wildlife-lovers, with several outstanding nature preserves close by, including the world-renowned Everglades National Park.

Naples is a great base for delving into the western fringes of the Everglades National Park. The preserve's vast expanses of sawgrass prairie plains and sun-dappled mangroves harbor countless species, including bald eagles, osprey, wading birds, sea turtles, manatees, and dolphins—plus the notorious American alligator.

WAILEA

South Maui's leeward coast is one of Hawai'i's top destinations for activities in, on, and near the water. And at the center of it all is Wailea, an exclusive resort that boasts luxury facilities and some of the finest crescent beaches in the world. Sheltered by the towering bulk of the Haleakalā volcano, Wailea's sunny shoreline has calm seas ideal for swimming, snorkeling, and wreck-diving, while on land there are pretty coastal walks that offer great views of the shimmering blue Pacific Ocean.

The Haleakalā volcano is one of the unmissable attractions on Hawai'i's second-largest island. It is thought to have erupted more than 200 years ago, and is still considered to be active today. Standing at its summit is a breathtaking experience, because of both the high altitude and the magnificent view of the entire volcano.

PALM SPRINGS

With first-class hotels, countless sparkling swimming pools and luxury golf courses, Palm Springs is a monument to leisure in an awesome setting. Bound by the snow-capped San Jacinto mountains, this Californian desert city was settled in the 1850s and soon became a thriving health spa and winter resort for the rich and famous. Today, it is just as alluring to both celebrities and sunseekers, who come to enjoy its cobalt skies and relaxed lifestyle.

Outdoor attractions abound in Palm Springs: the San Jacinto mountains are crisscrossed with superb hiking and riding trails (plus some great skiing trails in winter); the Aerial Tramway affords stunning views from the top of Mount San Jacinto; and nearby lie the Indian Canyons—four natural palm oases set in spectacular gorges.

SCOTTSDALE

In the heart of the Sonoran desert lies this unique town, steeped in classic Western style and Native American history. Located on the outskirts of Phoenix, Arizona, this winter retreat attracts artists, golfers, and hikers with its warm climate and desert setting. It's a cultural and entertainment paradise too, with upscale shops, restaurants, and galleries. After dark, its hip clubs and bars burst into life, transforming this quiet town into a glamorous party playground.

Golf is big business in Scottsdale. With more than 200 world-class courses in and around the city, such as the renowned Boulders Club and Troon North, this town is one of the best golfing destinations in the world. Superbly groomed links, top-level instruction, and a perfect climate combine to make Scottsdale a desert golfer's dream.

SARASOTA

This affluent waterfront town is the thriving cultural hub of Florida. Artists and writers are drawn to Sarasota for its pure light and peaceful atmosphere, while culture-vultures devour the offerings of its excellent museums, galleries, opera houses, and theaters. Here, life can be indulgently lazy—the town's antique stores, cafés, bars, and restaurants are designed for lingering, while the powdery white-sand beaches of the nearby barrier islands are endlessly inviting.

Much of Sarasota's wealth is credited to the millionaire circus owner John Ringling, who invested his fortune in the area. His legacy is best seen at the Ringling Museum Complex, which houses a collection of European art, a Circus Museum, and the Ca'd'Zan—his opulent home, which is modeled on a Venetian palace.

finding paradise

"...Turn the island experience from wishful thinking into reality...embrace the sun and surf, and add a touch of tropical fun to your life..."

living the good life

Tommy Bahama®

SCENTS OF THE TROPICS BEACH
FINDS OUTDOOR LIVING SOUNDS
OF PARADISE ISLAND INSPIRED
WEDDING BEACH PICNIC NIGHTTIME
ON THE BEACH BRINGING HOME
PARADISE SCENTS OF THE TROPICS
BEACH FINDS OUTDOOR LIVING
SOUNDS OF PARADISE ISLAND
INSPIRED WEDDING BEACH PICNIC
NIGHTTIME ON THE BEACH BRINGING
HOME PARADISE SCENTS OF THE
TROPICS BEACH FINDS OUTDOOR
LIVING SOUNDS OF PARADISE
ISLAND INSPIRED WEDDING
BEACH PICNIC NIGHTTIME ON THE
BEACH BRINGING HOME PARADISE
SCENTS OF THE TROPICS BEACH
FINDS OUTDOOR LIVING SOUNDS
OF PARADISE ISLAND INSPIRED
WEDDING BEACH PICNIC NIGHTTIME
ON THE BEACH BRINGING HOME

bringing home
paradise

THAT TROPICAL touch can be brought into your home wherever you live.
Go for furniture crafted in rich, exotic wood, bamboo, and cane. Festoon sofas,
armchairs, and beds in sultry oriental or vibrant Caribbean prints. Stay cool with
plantation-style ceiling fans and maybe pick up an interesting curio, such as
an old sea-captain's chest, filled with fascinating antique maps and instruments
that were once used to steer a safe passage across the oceans of the world.

1. Plantation-style ceiling fan in teak, cane, and brass. **2.** Low-key wood-framed sofa. **3.** Old "colonial" bedstead. **4.** Model of an old Caribbean sailing vessel. **5.** Antique sea-captain's instrument chest. **6.** Mahogany mirror frame and chest, topped with clear glass jars of seashells and beach pebbles.

1

2

3

4

5

6

scents of the tropics

THE SENSUAL, heady perfume of flowers and fruit alone can encapsulate that perfect tropical moment. Delicate, vibrant, spicy, floral, fruity, or sweet, there is a fragrance to match every mood. Even when fresh blooms or produce are in short supply, simply lighting a scented candle will release the seductive scent of paradise into every corner of your home.

1. Soft lights and fresh air or the scent of nature make for a perfect romantic dinner. **2.** Table decoration of fragrant rose petals, scattered into a bowl of lightly perfumed water. **3.** Arrangement of richly aromatic tropical fruits. **4. & 5.** Scented candles. **6.** The sweet-scented *Phalaenopsis* orchid, most fragrant in the evening.

beach finds

A RELAXING walk along the beach can lead you to a treasure trove of natural finds with which to adorn your home. Shells, dried seaweed, driftwood, and even the remains of old ships can all be salvaged and crafted into stunning collages, sculptures, and table decorations. Bring that holiday feeling into your living room by capturing the colors of the tropics in a fresh, new decorative scheme. Gather up, photograph, or simply take note of whatever catches your eye…then let your imagination be your guide.

1. Speckled conch shells from a Florida beach. **2.** "Carpet" of bladder wrack, cast ashore at low tide. **3.** Spider conch, found in the coastal shallows and coral beds of the Pacific. **4.** Anchor, salvaged from an old Panamanian trading vessel. **5** Sea urchin shells. **6.** Wreck of an abandoned fishing vessel. **7.** Sea kale floating at the water's edge. **8.** Driftwood, bleached by the tropical sun.

outdoor living

LIVING IN the tropics with year-round sunshine and soft, warm ocean breezes means a lifestyle where indoor and outdoor activities merge almost seamlessly. Whether you just want to relax and soak up the sunshine, barbecue some freshly caught fish on the beach, or enjoy fine dining on a balcony or garden overlooking the ocean, island life is at its best lived under an open sky.

1. Tropical wood deck chair for complete relaxation.
2. Simple rope hammock slung across the corner of a veranda. **3.** A spray of pink, scented orchids.
4. Outdoor tableware for special occasions.
5. Cooling off before a leisurely shore lunch.
6. Fine dining alfresco. **7.** Tommy Bahama tumbler, designed to keep your drink cooler for longer. **8.** Barbecue tools.

sounds of
paradise

FROM SOFT sambas and cool jazz to hot Latin rhythms and
Brazilian beats, the music of the tropics comes directly from the soul.
Guitars, drums, and violins sing out in the clear, warm air to create
the perfect party mood. Chill out, relax, and dance into the sunset.

1. Cuban street fiddler 2. Flamenco, imported into Latin America from Spain. 3. Thumb piano, used to accompany vocals in the Caribbean and parts of Africa. 4. Maracas from North Africa (left) and Spain (right). 5. Beating in the sunset on a Hawaiian beach. 6. African conga. 7. Acoustic guitar 8. Rhythms and melodies of paradise, captured on CD by Tommy Bahama.

island inspired
wedding

THAT SPECIAL day deserves a truly romantic setting, so why not choose to exchange vows on the golden, sun-kissed sands of a tropical beach? The light filtering through the swaying palms, the soft ocean breeze, and the gentle ebb and flow of the waves all combine to create a small corner of paradise. Keep it low-key but elegant. Match a casual gown with a single strand of pearls. Choose scented island flowers for the bridal bouquet and table. Dine on the freshest local seafood, simply prepared, matched with exotic cocktails and the very best Champagne.

1. Curaçao cocktail. 2. Simple yet elegant beach wedding attire. 3. Aromatic island orchids for the bridal bouquet. 4. Fresh shrimp canapé. 5. Floral table decoration with scented candles. 6. Classic pearl necklace. 7. A wedding venue in a perfect setting. 8. Palm trees decorated with fragrant flowers.

•beach picnic

ESCAPE TO the soothing rhythms of beach life and leave your cares behind. Grab a blanket and some cushions, pack a hamper, and head down to the shore for a leisurely day with family and friends. Stuffed tortillas, slices of piña colada cake, salads, and prepared skewers and steaks, ready to toss on a beach barbecue, make for an easy-to-serve feast.

1. Chilled beer, straight from the bottle with a wedge of fresh lime. **2.** Perfect picnic food. **3.** Canvas beach tote, packed and ready for action. **4.** Caddy of beer glasses. **5.** A fresh and tasty lunch, served up with a fruity red wine. **6.** Traditional fishing boats, Praia Combuco, Brazil.

nighttime on the beach

GRAB A lantern and wander down to the shore at sunset to soak up the peace and tranquility of the tropical night. Meditate, enjoy a moment of romance, or just mellow out and chat with friends around the glowing embers of a campfire. Linger as the sinking sun sends ripples of gold and red out over the still, black blanket of the nighttime ocean.

1. Practising the ancient martial art of *capoeira* on a Brazilian beach. **2.** Around the campfire on Newport Beach, California. **3.** Lying in a hammock—an unbeatable way to relax. **4.** Twirling fire poi on Samara Beach, Guanacaste, Costa Rica. **5.** Candle-lit torches, staked out along the shoreline.

living an active life

Tommy Bahama®

AILING BEACH GAMES WATER SPOR
OLF SAILING BEACH GAMES WATER
PORTS GOLF SAILING BEACH GAME
ATER SPORTS GOLF SAILING BEAC
AMES WATER SPORTS GOLF SAILIN
EACH GAMES WATER SPORTS GOLF
AILING BEACH GAMES GOLF SAILIN
ATER SPORTS GOLF SAILING BEAC
AMES WATER SPORTS BEACH GAME
OLF SAILING BEACH GAMES WATE
PORTS GOLF SAILING BEACH GAME
ATER SPORTS GOLF SAILING BEAC
AMES WATER SPORTS GOLF SAILIN
EACH GAMES WATER SPORTS GOLF
AILING BEACH GAMES WATER SPOR
OLF SAILING BEACH GAMES WATE
PORTS GOLF SAILING BEACH GAME
AILING BEACH GAMES GOLF SAILIN
EACH GAMES WATER SPORTS GOLF
AILING BEACH GAMES WATER SPOR
OLF SAILING WATER SPORTS GOLF

beach games

BE PLAYFUL. Join in the action. The beach isn't just for lying around, soaking up the sun. Long, open stretches of soft sand make an ideal setting for an impromptu soccer match, or even a kite-flying competition. Make new friends over a game of volleyball or bocce. Then, as evening approaches, wind things down with a leisurely card game over a round of cooling cocktails, or simply play tic-tac-toe in the damp sand.

1. Colorful kite. **2.** Game of beach tic-tac-toe. **3.** Tommy Bahama® playing cards. **4.** Beach cricket stumps. **5.** Metal bocce. **6.** Getting together over a game of volleyball.

water sports

THE THRILLS and spills of the surf are there for everyone to enjoy—both expert and novice alike. It's easy to experience the fun and excitement of the ocean in the clean, clear waters of the tropics. Watersports centers, offering instruction and a helping hand at all levels, abound at most island resorts, so be bold, step into the waves, and discover a whole new world.

1. Scuba diver, exploring the magical, hidden world of the ocean bed. **2.** Kite boarding. **3.** Welcoming sign at one of Hawai'i's many surf centers. **4.** Diving into a wave. **5.** Body boarding. **6.** Taking off on a wakeboard. **7.** Sea-kayaking and snorkeling on a coral reef.

golf

ENDLESS SUNSHINE, soft ocean breezes, and lush greenery make the islands of the tropics a paradise for the golfing enthusiast. Take in breathtaking ocean views and savor some of the very best that nature has to offer, as you fine-tune your game and lower your handicap. Then to round off a perfect day, relax in the opulent comfort of the clubhouse over a drink or a gourmet dinner.

1. Teeing off. 2. Sunset over the links.
3. Opulent clubhouse in the Art Deco district of Palm Beach, Florida. 4. Following the ball across the green. 5 Colonial-style clubhouse in the Caribbean. 6. Checking the score over a round of soothing, end-of-game cocktails.

sailing

REDISCOVER YOUR spirit of adventure as you glide through pristine, azure blue waters, the warm breeze gently brushing against your face and through your hair. Steering a course over the high seas in a top-end yacht is by far the best way of exploring the multitude of secluded, tranquil bays and unspoilt islands that make the tropics such an earthly paradise.

1. Taking control at the helm. **2.** Finely crafted brass winch, with the Latin inscription *faventibus ventis* ("may the winds be favorable".) **3.** Yachts moored in the picturesque harbor of Hopetown in the sunny Bahamas. **4.** Trimming the sail. **5.** Cruising through the waters of the Atlantic Ocean. **6.** At anchor in a secluded bay, enjoying the warm, sunlit waters.

island-inspired cuisine

"Smooth, creamy, fiery, sharp...Let the vibrant and varied flavors of the tropics bring a fresh twist to that special occasion or impromptu gathering, or even to simple, everyday family meals. Get together, relax, and savor the taste of paradise..."

little luxuries

COOPER ISLAND CRAB

BISQUE TORTOLA

TORTILLA SOUP BIG

ISLAND GOAT CHEESE

CRAB & AVOCADO

"SORT OF" SUSHI

CRAB CALLOWAY

TOMMY'S WORLD

FAMOUS COCONUT

SHRIMP RED, WHITE,

AND BLEU ARUBA

ARUGULA SALAD

TAHITIAN TUNA SALAD

COOPER ISLAND CRAB

COOPER ISLAND CRAB BISQUE

INGREDIENTS

6oz unsalted butter
2 tablespoons all-purpose flour
6 cups whipping cream
1 stick fresh celery, trimmed and finely diced
1 medium carrot, peeled and cut into matchstick strips
1 small red onion, finely chopped

SERVES 6

Melt 2oz butter in a medium saucepan. Stir in the flour until well blended. Cook, stirring, until the mixture is a light golden color. Meanwhile, warm 4 cups whipping cream over low heat in a separate pan. Stir cream into the flour mixture and cook over medium heat, stirring continuously, until the mixture thickens and is smooth. Set aside.

In a medium saucepan, melt 1oz butter. Add the celery, carrot, red onion, shallots, garlic, and thyme and cook over medium heat until all the vegetables are tender. Remove from the heat and stir in 1 cup dry sherry. Return to the heat and cook gently, stirring and scraping any browned bits from the base of the pan, for 2–3 minutes to burn off any alcohol.

In a small bowl, blend the Minor's shrimp base with the water until dissolved. Stir into the pan of cooked vegetables and bring to a boil over medium heat. Lower the heat and simmer gently, covered, for 20 minutes. Pre-heat the oven to 350°F.

Strain the vegetable mixture through a fine-mesh strainer into the cream mixture and stir well to blend. Add the Tabasco sauce and the remainder of the whipping cream. Return the mixture to a boil, reduce the heat and simmer very gently, covered, for 20 minutes or until the mixture coats the back of a spoon. Remove from the heat.

While the soup is simmering, place the soft cracker bread strips on a baking sheet, brush with the olive oil and sprinkle lightly with salt and pepper. Bake in hot oven for 8–10 minutes, until crisp. Set aside and keep warm.

Cut the remaining butter into small cubes and stir into hot soup mixture, a few cubes at a time until incorporated. Stir in the remaining sherry, then fold in the crabmeat. Heat through gently and serve, garnished with baby arugula leaves and accompanied with the warm strips of crisp cracker bread.

2 shallots, finely chopped

4 cloves garlic, finely chopped

5–6 sprigs fresh thyme, chopped

1½ cups dry sherry

¼ cup Minor's® shrimp base

1 cup water

½ teaspoon Tabasco® sauce

1 round soft cracker bread (lahvosh), cut into 6 x 3-inch long strips

1 tablespoon olive oil

salt

freshly ground black pepper

6oz lump crabmeat

baby arugula, to garnish

TORTOLA TORTILLA SOUP

INGREDIENTS

½ cup olive oil
4oz butter
2 medium onions, finely chopped
1 small green bell pepper, deseeded and finely chopped
6 cloves garlic, finely chopped

SERVES 6

Heat the olive oil and butter in a large saucepan over medium heat. Add the onions, pepper, and garlic and cook until tender and golden brown. In a small bowl, combine the flour, ground tortillas, chili powder, cumin, salt, black pepper, and cayenne pepper. Stir the flour mixture into the cooked vegetables. Add the chopped cilantro and cook over medium heat for 10–12 minutes, stirring constantly, until the mixture resembles toasted graham crackers. Remove from the heat.

Blend in the chicken stock, a little at a time, until all of it is well incorporated. Return the mixture to medium heat and bring to a boil. Lower the heat and leave to simmer gently for 40 minutes. Pour into a blender or food processor and process until smooth.

Return the soup mixture to a clean saucepan, heat through, and stir in the grilled diced chicken. Serve immediately, garnishing each serving with a drizzle of lime sour cream, a few fried tortilla strips, and a few sprigs of fresh cilantro.

3 tablespoons all-purpose flour

2 large corn tortillas, cut into small strips and finely ground in a food processor

1½ teaspoons chili powder

1½ teaspoons ground cumin

1½ teaspoons salt

½ teaspoon coarsely ground black pepper

¼ teaspoon cayenne pepper

1 tablespoon finely chopped fresh cilantro

2 quarts chicken stock

10oz skinless chicken breast, grilled and diced

1 recipe quantity Lime Sour Cream (see page 128)

1 recipe quantity Fried Tortilla Strips (see page 132)

sprigs of fresh cilantro, to garnish

PETIZERS

BIG ISLAND GOAT CHEESE
arm macadamia nut encrusted goat cheese served with mango
Tommy's flatbread and a sweet soy glaze.
11.50

OMMY'S WORLD-FAMOUS COCONUT SHRIMP
Crispy coconut encrusted jumbo shrimp served with
papaya-mango chutney and Asian slaw. .
17.00

LOKI-LOKI TUNA POKE•
poleon layered with freshly made guacamol.
ved with Tommy's flatbread

BIG ISLAND GOAT CHEESE

SERVES 6

Pre-heat the oven to 350°F. Place the strips of soft cracker bread on a baking sheet, brush with the olive oil and sprinkle lightly with salt and pepper. Bake in the oven for 8–10 minutes, until crisp. Set aside.

Shape the goat cheese into six 3-inch rounds. Roll each cheese round in the toasted and chopped macadamia nuts to coat well. Press the nuts gently onto the cheese to make sure that they adhere.

Heat the clarified butter or canola oil in a large skillet over medium heat. Add the prepared cheese rounds and cook for 1½ minutes on each side.

While the cheese rounds are cooking, place about a tablespoon of mango salsa on each serving plate. Top with a round of just-cooked goat cheese. Drizzle generously with sweet soy glaze and garnish with some baby arugula.

Serve immediately, accompanied by strips of crisp cracker bread.

INGREDIENTS

6 rounds soft cracker bread *(lahvosh)*, each cut into 6 x 3-inch long strips

1 tablespoon olive oil

salt

freshly ground black pepper

1lb 4oz soft goat cheese

½ cup macadamia nuts, toasted and finely chopped

2 tablespoons clarified butter, or canola oil

1 recipe quantity Mango Salsa *(see page 142)*

1 recipe quantity Sweet Soy Glaze *(see page 148)*

baby arugula, to garnish

CRAB AND AVOCADO "SORT OF" SUSHI

MAKES 16 ROLLS

Trim the ends of the zucchini or squash. Using a sharp vegetable peeler, slice the zucchini or squash lengthwise into wide flat "ribbons." Discard the first and last slices and the seedy section in the middle to leave 32 ribbons. Set aside.

Drain the crabmeat well in a colander, pressing with the back of a spoon to remove most of the liquid. Pat dry with paper towels and place in a mixing bowl. Stir in the mayonnaise, wasabi paste, and salt. Set aside. Cut the avocado into 16 strips.

Working on a clean surface, take two zucchini ribbons and lay one on top of the other. Place a slightly rounded teaspoon of the crab mixture at one end of the doubled zucchini ribbon. Top with a strip of avocodo, a few shreds of carrot, and a basil leaf. Roll up and secure with a toothpick. Repeat with the remaining ingredients to make a total of 16 rolls.

Arrange the rolls on a serving platter. Serve immediately or, if preferred, cover and chill for up to 30 minutes before serving.

INGREDIENTS

2 medium zucchini or yellow summer squash

5oz cooked lump crabmeat

1 tablespoon mayonnaise

1 teaspoon wasabi paste

pinch salt

½ medium avocado, peeled and stoned

1 large carrot, coarsely shredded

16 small fresh basil leaves

CRAB CALLOWAY

INGREDIENTS

1¼lb lump crabmeat

½ small red onion, finely chopped

1 small yellow onion, finely chopped

1 small green onion, finely chopped

1 egg, lightly beaten

SERVES 6

In a large bowl, combine the crabmeat with the red, yellow, and green onions, plus the egg, flour, 2 tablespoons panko crumbs, 1½ teaspoons Old Bay seasoning, salt, pepper, and celery salt. Take care not to break up the crabmeat. Shape the mixture into 12 round cakes.

In a shallow dish, combine the remaining panko crumbs and shredded coconut with the remaining Old Bay seasoning. Roll the crab cakes in this crumb mixture to coat well and set aside.

Heat the clarified butter in a large skillet over medium heat. Add half the prepared crab cakes and cook for about 3–5 minutes on each side until golden brown. Remove from the pan and drain well on paper towels. Set aside and keep warm. Repeat with the remaining crab cakes.

Spoon some sweet chili mustard sauce in the center of each serving plate. Top with a generous spoonful of Asian slaw, then place two warm crab cakes against the slaw. Garnish with baby arugula leaves and serve immediately.

3 tablespoons all-purpose flour

6 tablespoons panko (Japanese-style) breadcrumbs

1¾ teaspoons Old Bay® seasoning

1 teaspoon salt

1 teaspoon freshly ground black pepper

1 teaspoon celery salt

¼ cup shredded coconut

2 tablespoons clarified butter

1 recipe quantity Sweet Chili Mustard Sauce *(see page 128)*

1 recipe quantity Asian Slaw *(see page 143)*

baby arugula, to garnish

TOMMY'S WORLD FAMOUS COCONUT SHRIMP

SERVES 6

Place the beer, 1 cup flour, eggs, sugar, salt, and pepper in a large bowl and mix well to form a batter. Transfer to a shallow dish. Place the remaining flour in another shallow dish and the shredded coconut in a third shallow dish.

Dip the shrimp in the dish of flour to coat well, shaking off any excess. Then dip in the batter, allowing to drain for a second, then into the shredded coconut, pressing gently so that the coconut adheres to the shrimp. Set aside.

Heat the oil in a deep pan, until hot enough to brown a small cube of bread in about 30 seconds. Cook the shrimp in small batches in the hot oil for about 3 minutes, or until golden brown and opaque. Remove from the oil, drain on paper towels, and set aside and keep warm.

Place a generous spoonful of Asian slaw in the center of each serving plate. Arrange shrimp around the slaw and serve immediately with a small ramekin of mango chutney.

INGREDIENTS

1¼ cups beer

1⅔ cups all-purpose flour

2 eggs

¼ cup sugar

1 teaspoon salt

¼ teaspoon freshly ground black pepper

⅔ cup shredded coconut

1lb peeled and deveined raw medium shrimp

oil for deep-fat frying

1 recipe quantity Asian Slaw *(see page 143)*

mango chutney, to serve

RED, WHITE, AND BLEU

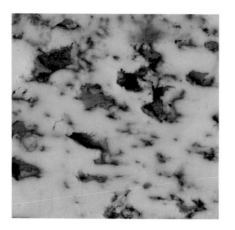

SERVES 6

Place the sliced red onion in a bowl of ice water and leave to stand for about 10 minutes. Drain and set aside.

Divide the romaine lettuce between six serving plates. Top with chopped tomato, then sprinkle salt and pepper to taste over the tomatoes. Drizzle balsamic vinaigrette around the outside edge of the lettuce. Spoon a generous portion of blue cheese dressing in the center of the tomatoes, then sprinkle with some crumbled blue cheese. Finally top with a generous sprinkling of the prepared red and green onion, and serve.

INGREDIENTS

1 large red onion, thinly sliced

3 heart of romaine lettuces, roughly chopped

2 large tomatoes, coarsely chopped

salt

freshly ground black pepper

1 recipe quantity Balsamic Vinaigrette *(see page 149)*

1 recipe quantity Blue Cheese Dressing *(see page 149)*

9oz Maytag® blue cheese, crumbled

10–12 green onions, sliced

ARUBA ARUGULA SALAD

SERVES 6

Place the cracker meal and Jamaican jerk seasoning in a shallow dish and mix to combine thoroughly. Season the shrimp and scallops with salt and pepper, then dip in the cracker meal mixture to coat well. Set aside.

Heat the oil in a large skillet over medium heat until just beginning to smoke. Add the prepared shrimp and scallops and sear until opaque and lightly browned. Remove from the pan and drain on paper towels. Set aside and keep warm.

Wipe out the skillet, then pour in the tamarind vinaigrette and heat gently until just warm. Pour the warm vinaigrette into a large bowl, add the arugula leaves and toss well to coat. Divide the dressed arugula between six serving plates. Place three cooked shrimp and two cooked scallops around each serving of arugula. Top with slices of papaya and a sprinkling of chopped peanuts. Serve immediately.

INGREDIENTS

1 cup cracker meal

2 tablespoons Jamaican jerk seasoning

18 raw medium shrimp, peeled and deveined

12 medium scallops

salt

freshly ground black pepper

4 tablespoons olive oil

1 recipe quantity Tamarind Vinaigrette *(see page 148)*

1¼lb arugula leaves

1 medium papaya, peeled and sliced

¼ cup chopped peanuts

TAHITIAN TUNA SALAD

INGREDIENTS

1½ tablespoons blackened seasoning

1½lb Ahi tuna steaks

1 tablespoon olive oil

8oz baby arugula leaves

8oz baby spinach leaves

SERVES 6

Place the blackened seasoning in a shallow dish. Add the tuna steaks and turn to coat well with the seasoning on all sides.

Heat the oil over medium-high heat in a large skillet. Add the tuna steaks and cook for 3–4 minutes on each side, or until the fish is beginning to flake and brown, but is still pink in the center. Alternatively, grill the tuna on a lightly oiled griddle. Remove from the pan or griddle and chill until ready to serve.

In a large mixing bowl, combine the arugula, spinach, and carrot. Add the lilioki vinaigrette and toss until the leaves and carrot are well coated. Season to taste with salt and pepper.

Slice the chilled tuna thinly and divide between six serving plates, arranged in an arc around one side of the plate. Place a mound of the dressed salad on each plate and top with a scattering of fried wonton strips. Drizzle some sweet soy glaze and wasabi aioli over the tuna, then sprinkle the tuna with sesame seeds. Place a small ramekin of soy sauce, with a dollop of wasabi on its rim, on each plate and serve.

2 medium carrots, peeled and cut into matchstick strips

1 recipe quantity Lilioki Vinaigrette *(see page 147)*

salt

freshly ground black pepper

⅓ cup wonton wrappers, cut into thin strips and fried until crisp

⅓ cup Sweet Soy Glaze *(see page 148)*

1 recipe quantity Wasabi Aioli *(see page 141)*

1 tablespoon black and white sesame seeds

soy sauce

wasabi paste

shore lunch

Tommy Bahama

T. CROIX CHOPPED
ALAD ST. BART'S
LT HABANA CABANA
ORK SANDWICH
OMMY'S GREAT
IG CRISPY FISH
ANDWICH ST. CROIX
HOPPED SALAD ST.
ART'S BLT HABANA
ABANA PORK
ANDWICH TOMMY'S
REAT BIG CRISPY
ISH SANDWICH ST.
ROIX CHOPPED

ST. CROIX CHOPPED SALAD

SERVES 6

Heat a large skillet over medium-high heat. Add the bacon and cook for 3–5 minutes, or until crisp. Remove from the pan, drain on paper towels, crumble and set aside. Add the chicken to the hot skillet and cook over medium-high heat for 10–15 minutes, turning once, or until cooked through and lightly golden. Chop up roughly and set aside.

Place the salad greens, crumbled bacon, macadamia nuts, and corn in a large mixing bowl. Add the honey lime dressing and toss to mix well.

Divide the salad mixture between six chilled plates. Top with a scattering of garlic croutons, diced tomato, chopped apple, blue cheese, and some of the chopped, cooked chicken. Serve immediately.

INGREDIENTS

12 slices bacon

1lb skinless, boneless chicken breasts

5oz torn mixed salad greens

1½ cups macadamia nuts, chopped

¾ cup fresh corn kernels, blanched

1 recipe quantity Honey Lime Dressing *(see page 146)*

2 cups pre-prepared garlic croutons

6 large tomatoes, peeled, deseeded, and diced

3 Granny Smith apples, cored and chopped

1 cup crumbled Maytag® blue cheese

ST. BART'S BLT

SERVES 6

Place the shrimp in a shallow dish. Drizzle with the lemon garlic oil and sprinkle with salt and pepper. Mix to coat the shrimp well. Thread the shrimp onto skewers, then grill on a medium-hot, well-oiled grill, or over medium coals, for 5–8 minutes or until opaque, turning once. Remove the shrimp from the skewers, set aside and keep warm. Cook the bacon in a skillet on medium-high heat for 3–5 minutes, or until crisp. Drain on paper towels and set aside.

Spread butter on one side of each bread slice. Lightly toast both sides of the bread on the hot grill or coals.

Place a toasted bread slice, buttered-side down, on each of six warm serving plates. Spread each generously with garlic aioli, then top with two lettuce leaves, two tomato slices, five cooked shrimp, and two crispy bacon slices. Cover with another toasted bread slice. Use cocktail sticks to hold the sandwiches together. Slice each sandwich in half and serve with pasta salad.

INGREDIENTS

30 raw medium shrimp, peeled and deveined

⅓ cup Lemon Garlic Oil *(see page 127)*, or olive oil

½ teaspoon salt

¼ teaspoon freshly ground black pepper

12 slices bacon

½ cup unsalted butter, softened

12 slices sourdough bread

⅔ cup Garlic Aioli *(see page 141)*

12 crisp green lettuce leaves

12 thin slices tomato

1 recipe quantity Pasta Salad *(see page 144)*

HABANA CABANA PORK SANDWICH

SERVES 6

Place the shredded pork and blackberry brandy BBQ sauce in a large saucepan and heat through.

While the pork is heating, slice the sandwich rolls in half and lightly toast each piece on both sides. Place half a toasted roll on each of six serving plates. Mound a generous helping of the warm pork on top, then top with onion strings. Top each serving with the remaining half of each toasted roll.

Quickly toss together the Asian slaw and crisp wonton strips and add a generous helping of this mixture to each serving platter, alongside the sandwich. Serve immediately with freshly cooked French fries.

INGREDIENTS

2lb lean pork, broiled or pan fried and shredded

1 recipe quantity Blackberry Brandy BBQ Sauce *(see page 126)*

6 large sandwich rolls

1 recipe quantity Onion Strings *(see page 131)*

1 recipe quantity Asian Slaw *(see page 143)*

¾ cup wonton wrappers, cut into thin strips and fried until crisp

French fries, to serve

TOMMY'S GREAT BIG CRISPY FISH SANDWICH

INGREDIENTS

sunflower or peanut oil for deep-fat frying

3 cups dry pancake or biscuit mix

1 recipe quantity Beer Batter *(see page 127)*

6 sea bass fillets, about 6oz each

SERVES 6

Heat the oil in a deep-sided pan until it is hot enough to brown a small cube of bread in about 30 seconds.

Meanwhile, place the dry pancake or biscuit mix in a shallow dish and pour the beer batter into another large shallow dish. Dip each sea bass fillet first into the dry batter mix until well coated, shaking off any excess, then into the beer batter. Fry the fish in the hot oil for 3–4 minutes, or until it floats to the top and is golden brown. The flesh should flake when tested with a fork.

While the fish is cooking, lightly toast the hamburger bun halves on both sides. Place the bottom half of a bun on each of six serving plates. Top with a piece of freshly cooked fish, then a helping of honey roasted onions, and finally the bun top. Place a lettuce leaf, tomato slice and pickle spear on each plate. Sprinkle salt and pepper over the tomato. Serve immediately, accompanied by a small ramekin of the island tartar sauce and freshly cooked French fries.

6 hamburger buns, sliced in half horizontally

1 recipe quantity Honey Roasted Onions *(see page 131)*

6 crisp green lettuce leaves

6 thin slices tomato

6 pickle spears

salt

freshly ground black pepper

1 recipe quantity Island Tartar Sauce *(see page 125)*

French fries, to serve

easy breezy weeknights

Tommy Bahama®

TRINIDAD TUNA
SANIBEL STUFFED
CHICKEN PORT-AU-
PRINCE BONE-IN PORK
CHOP TRINIDAD TUNA
SANIBEL STUFFED
CHICKEN PORT-AU-
PRINCE BONE-IN PORK
CHOP TRINIDAD TUNA
SANIBEL STUFFED
CHICKEN PORT-AU-
PRINCE BONE-IN PORK
CHOP TRINIDAD TUNA
SANIBEL STUFFED

TRINIDAD TUNA

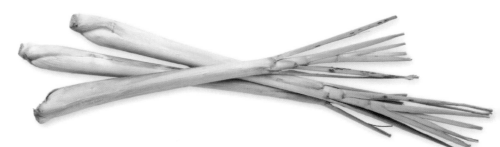

SERVES 6

In a shallow dish, mix together the panko breadcrumbs, lemongrass, and fresh cilantro. Season each tuna steak with salt and pepper, then dip in the panko crumb mixture until well coated on all sides.

In a large skillet, heat the peanut oil over medium-high heat. Add the prepared tuna steaks and cook for 3–4 minutes on each side, or until the fish is lightly browned and is beginning to flake but is still pink in the center. Remove from the pan and drain on paper towels.

Divide the hot baby bok choy and shitakes between six warm serving plates. Top each serving with a freshly cooked tuna steak. Spoon some sweet chili glaze around the vegetables, then drizzle some cilantro oil around the edge of the glaze. Put some wasabi paste and pickled ginger on each plate and garnish the tuna with baby arugula leaves and a sprinkling of sesame seeds, if desired. Serve immediately.

INGREDIENTS

¾ cup panko (Japanese-style) breadcrumbs

2 tablespoons finely chopped lemongrass

1 tablespoon finely chopped fresh cilantro

6 Ahi tuna steaks, about 8oz each

salt and freshly ground black pepper

2 tablespoons peanut oil

1 recipe quantity Baby Bok Choy and Shitakes *(see page 133)*

1 recipe quantity Sweet Chili Glaze (see page 139)

¼ cup Cilantro Oil *(see page 139)*

2 tablespoons wasabi paste

2 tablespoons pickled ginger

baby arugula leaves, to garnish

black and white sesame seeds, to garnish (optional)

SANIBEL STUFFED CHICKEN

SERVES 6

Place plastic wrap over each chicken breast and lightly pound with a mallet until about ¼ inch thick. Season with salt and pepper. Place a small portion of Alouette® cheese and some roasted red pepper strips on top of each piece of flattened chicken, then fold the chicken over to enclose the mixture. Use toothpicks to hold closed if necessary.

In a shallow dish, combine the panko breadcrumbs, Parmesan cheese, basil, and parsley. Place the flour in another shallow dish, and in a third shallow dish, place the half-and-half. Dip the stuffed chicken pieces, first in the flour, shaking off any excess, then in the half-and-half, and finally in the panko crumb mixture to coat completely.

Preheat the oven to 450°F. In a large, ovenproof skillet, heat the olive oil over medium-high heat. Add the prepared chicken in a single layer, then place the skillet in the hot oven and bake the chicken for 8 minutes. Remove from the oven, turn the chicken over, return to the oven and bake for a further 8 minutes, or until the chicken is thoroughly cooked through and golden brown, and cheese is beginning to ooze out of the middle.

About 3–4 minutes before the chicken is cooked, reheat the blanched broccolini.

Heat the roasted red pepper cream sauce and spoon a helping onto each of six warm serving plates. Top with a helping of hot broccolini, then a piece of cooked stuffed chicken. Serve immediately.

INGREDIENTS

6 skinless, boneless, chicken breasts, about 8oz each

salt and freshly ground black pepper

6oz Alouette® cheese

4 red bell peppers, roasted, deseeded, and cut into thin strips

¾ cup panko (Japanese-style) breadcrumbs

5oz Parmesan cheese, grated

3 tablespoons finely chopped fresh basil

3 tablespoons finely chopped fresh parsley

¾ cup all-purpose flour

1 cup half-and-half

2 tablespoons olive oil

1 recipe quantity Blanched Broccolini *(see page 134)*

1 recipe quantity Roasted Red Pepper Cream Sauce *(see page 130)*

PORT-AU-PRINCE BONE-IN PORK CHOP

SERVES 6

Grill the pork chops on a well-oiled, hot griddle, or over medium coals, for 16–20 minutes, turning once, until the meat is well browned and thoroughly cooked through. Season well with salt and pepper.

Divide the freshly prepared roasted garlic mashed potatoes between six warmed serving plates. Place one freshly cooked pork chop on each plate. Spoon some warm port wine demi-glace sauce over each chop, garnish with parsley sprigs and serve immediately.

INGREDIENTS

6 bone-in pork rib chops, about 14oz each

salt

freshly ground black pepper

1 recipe quantity Roasted Garlic Mashed Potatoes *(see page 138)*

1 recipe quantity Port Wine Demi-Glace Sauce *(see page 140)*

sprigs of fresh flat-leaf parsley, to garnish

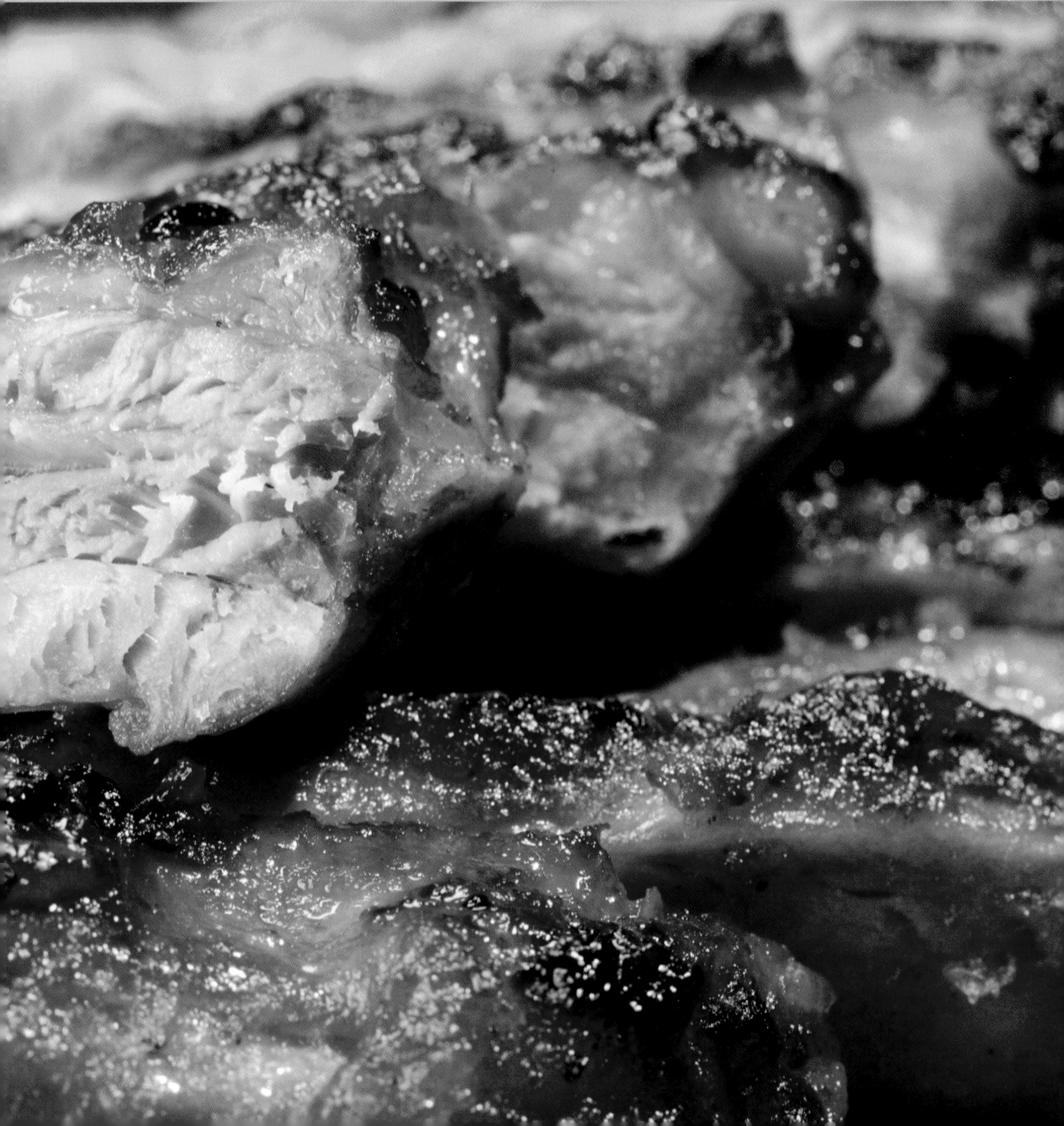

fine times with friends

Tommy Bahama®

MACADAMIA NUT-CRUSTED SNAPPER
TREASURE QUAY
AHI TUNA THE
ISLAND COWBOY
PINA COLADA CAKE
MACADAMIA NUT-CRUSTED SNAPPER
TREASURE QUAY
AHI TUNA THE
ISLAND COWBOY
PINA COLADA CAKE
MACADAMIA NUT-CRUSTED SNAPPER

MACADAMIA NUT-CRUSTED SNAPPER

SERVES 6

Pre-heat the oven to 350°F. Sprinkle the fish fillets generously with salt and pepper and set aside.

In a shallow dish, whisk together the egg yolks and water. Place the flour in another shallow dish and the macadamia nut crust mixture in a third shallow dish. Dip the seasoned fish fillets in the dish of flour until well coated, shaking to remove any excess flour. Then dip in the egg mixture and finally in the macadamia nut crust mixture to coat lightly. Set aside.

Heat half of the clarified butter or canola oil in a large skillet over medium heat. Add two fish fillets to the skillet and brown for 3 minutes on each side. Transfer the fish to a large, shallow baking dish. Repeat with the remaining fish fillets, adding more clarified butter or canola oil to the skillet as needed. Place the baking dish of fish in the hot oven for 4–5 minutes, or until the fish is cooked through. While the fish finishes cooking, heat about 1 tablespoon of the remaining oil in a large skillet over medium heat. Add the blanched broccolini and sauté gently to heat through.

Ladle some warm wasabi butter sauce onto each serving plate. Place some hot broccolini on top, then lay a freshly cooked fish fillet over the broccolini. Garnish with an orchid, if desired, and serve immediately.

INGREDIENTS

6 yellowtail snapper fillets, about 6oz each

salt

freshly ground black pepper

7 egg yolks

½ cup water

1½ cups all-purpose flour

1 recipe quantity Macadamia Nut Crust *(see page 145)*

8–10 tablespoons clarified butter or canola oil

1½ recipe quantity Blanched Broccolini *(see page 134)*

1 recipe quantity Wasabi Butter Sauce *(see page 125)*

edible orchids, to garnish (optional)

TREASURE QUAY
AHI TUNA

SERVES 6

Place the blackened seasoning in a shallow dish. Add the tuna steaks and turn to coat well with the seasoning on all sides. Heat the oil in a large skillet over medium-high heat. Add the tuna steaks and brown for 4 minutes on each side, or until the fish begins to flake but is still pink in the center. Remove from the skillet and leave to chill until ready to serve.

To serve, slice the tuna steaks thinly and divide between six serving plates, arranged in an arc around one side of the plate. Place a small mound of mixed salad greens in the center of each plate. Drizzle tamarind vinaigrette over the greens and tuna, and place a small portion of pickled ginger and wasabi paste on the side of each plate, together with a ramekin of soy sauce for dipping and some wonton crisps. Drizzle wasabi aioli over the tuna and serve.

INGREDIENTS

2 tablespoons blackened seasoning

1½lb Ahi tuna steaks

1 tablespoon olive oil

3–4oz mixed salad greens

1 recipe quantity Tamarind Vinaigrette *(see page 148)*

5 tablespoons pickled ginger

2 tablespoons wasabi paste

1 cup soy sauce

1 recipe quantity Wonton Crisps *(see page 132)*

1 recipe quantity Wasabi Aioli *(see page 141)*

THE ISLAND COWBOY

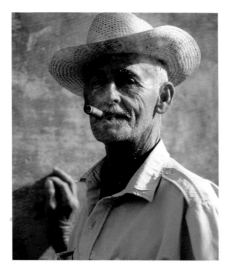

SERVES 6

Bring a large pan of water to a boil. Add a pinch of salt, then the asparagus spears and cook for 2–3 minutes. Drain and immediately plunge the asparagus into a bowl of ice water to chill and stop any further cooking. Drain well again and set aside.

Season the steaks with salt and pepper. Grill on a medium-hot griddle for 10–12 minutes (medium-rare) or 12–15 minutes (medium), turning once during cooking. When the steak is almost done, toss the asparagus in the lemon garlic oil, then grill on the hot griddle for 3–5 minutes, or until tender and lightly charred.

Ladle some warm port wine demi-glace sauce onto each serving plate. Place some freshly cooked asparagus spears and a steak on each plate, then sprinkle over the roasted garlic cloves and crumbled blue cheese. Serve immediately.

INGREDIENTS

salt

1¼lb fresh green asparagus spears, trimmed

6 beef *filet mignon* (tenderloin) steaks, about 8oz each

freshly ground black pepper

1 tablespoon Lemon Garlic Oil *(see page 127)* or olive oil

1 recipe quantity Port Wine Demi-Glace Sauce
   (see page 140)

1 recipe quantity Roasted Garlic Cloves *(see page 135)*

¾ cup crumbled Maytag® blue cheese

PIÑA COLADA CAKE

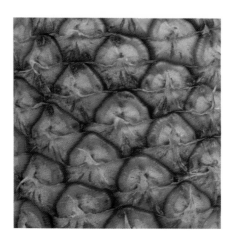

SERVES 6–8

Prepare and bake the cake mix according to the package directions, dividing the cake batter between two 9-inch, lightly greased cake pans. Remove from the oven and leave to cool in the pans for 10 minutes. Remove cakes from the pans and leave to cool completely on a wire rack. When cool, trim off the domed top of each cake, then slice each in half horizontally to make 4 cake layers in total.

Place one cake layer on a serving plate. Brush with some dark rum, then spread 1 cup of the sweetened whipped cream over the top, spreading smoothly. Spread one-third of the crushed pineapple over the cream, then top with another cake layer. Repeat twice more. Brush the top of the cake lightly with the remaining dark rum, then frost the top and the sides with the remaining sweetened whipped cream. Coat the frosted sides and top of the cake with the toasted coconut, leaving no bare spots. Chill until ready to serve. Serve sliced, with a small helping of sweetened whipped cream on the side, garnished with a fresh pineapple frond.

INGREDIENTS

1 box white cake mix

¼ Tommy Bahama Golden Sun® dark rum

1 recipe quantity Sweetened Whipped Cream *(see page 152)*

1 20-oz can crushed pineapple, drained

1 recipe quantity Toasted Coconut *(see page 153)*

fresh pineapple fronds, to decorate

soothing saturdays
and sundays

MAMA BAHAMA'S
CHICKEN SANDWICH
SANTIAGO SEA BASS
TOMMY'S RIB RACK
CAPTAIN COOK'S
BREAD PUDDING
BLACKBEARD'S
BUTTERSCOTCH
MAMA BAHAMA'S
CHICKEN SANDWICH
SANTIAGO SEA BASS
TOMMY'S RIB RACK
CAPTAIN COOK'S
BREAD PUDDING

MAMA BAHAMA'S CHICKEN SANDWICH

INGREDIENTS

1 cup olive oil

¼ cup fresh lemon juice

6 cloves garlic, finely chopped

1 tablespoon chicken stock

6–8 sprigs fresh rosemary, finely chopped

1 teaspoon finely chopped fresh parsley

SERVES 6

Prepare a marinade by placing the olive oil, lemon juice, garlic, chicken stock, rosemary, and parsley in a medium mixing bowl with a generous pinch of freshly ground black pepper and a pinch of crushed red chili pepper. Mix well to combine. Pour into a large shallow dish, add the chicken breasts, and turn to coat with the marinade. Cover with plastic wrap and place in the refrigerator to chill for at least 3 hours, but preferably overnight.

Remove the chicken from the dish, discarding any remaining marinade. Grill the chicken on a medium-hot grill or over medium coals for 12–15 minutes, turning once during the cooking time, until no longer pink. Season well with salt and pepper.

Just before the chicken is cooked, split the hamburger buns and toast lightly on both sides. Spread each bun top with half a tablespoon of jerk sauce and place on a serving plate. Arrange a lettuce leaf, a slice of seasoned tomato, and a pickle spear on top. Add a bun bottom to each serving plate and top with a freshly cooked piece of chicken. Place two slices of cheese on top of the chicken, then top with a generous helping of onion strings and drizzle with remaining jerk sauce and some garlic aioli. Serve immediately with a small bowl of pasta salad on the side.

freshly ground black pepper

crushed red chili pepper

6 skinless chicken breasts, about 6oz each

salt

6 hamburger buns

1 recipe quantity Jerk Sauce *(see page 129)*

6 crisp green lettuce leaves

6 thin slices tomato, lightly seasoned with salt and pepper

6 pickle spears

12 slices Monterey Jack cheese with jalapeño peppers

1 recipe quantity Onion Strings *(see page 131)*

3 tablespoons Garlic Aioli *(see page 141)*

1 recipe quantity Pasta Salad *(see page 144)*

SANTIAGO SEA BASS

SERVES 6

Pre-heat the oven to 450°F.

Bring a large pan of water to a boil. Add a pinch of salt, then the asparagus and cook for 2–3 minutes. Drain and immediately plunge the asparagus into a bowl of ice water to chill and stop further cooking. Drain again and set aside.

Place the olive oil in a large sauté pan and heat until sizzling. Turn the heat down to medium, add the sea bass fillets, skin-side down, and cook for about 2 minutes. Flip the sea bass over and transfer to a shallow baking dish. Cook in the hot oven for about 8–10 minutes, depending on the thickness of the fish. While the fish is cooking, heat the asparagus spears in a sauté pan for 5–6 minutes, or until tender, turning occasionally. Toss the cooked asparagus in the lemon garlic oil, then set aside and keep warm.

Divide the warm asparagus spears between six serving plates, all the tips pointing in the same direction. Place a cooked sea bass fillet on each asparagus serving, then top with about a tablespoon of the basil, olive, and walnut sauce. Garnish with a fresh basil leaf and a wedge of lemon. Serve immediately.

INGREDIENTS

salt

large bunch fresh green asparagus spears, about
1½lb, trimmed

1 tablespoon olive oil

6 sea bass fillets, about 8oz each

1 recipe quantity Lemon Garlic Oil *(see page 127)*

1 recipe quantity Basil, Olive, and Walnut Sauce
(see page 124)

6 leaves fresh basil

1 large lemon, cut into 6 wedges

TOMMY'S RIB RACK

SERVES 6

Pre-heat the oven to 350°F.

Place the brown sugar, Jamaican jerk seasoning, blackened seasoning, and salt in a small bowl and mix to combine well. Lightly coat each side of the rib racks with this mixture. Arrange the racks in a single layer in a large roasting pan.

In a medium bowl, whisk together the Coca Cola, water, liquid smoke, and Worcestershire sauce. Pour the mixture over the ribs. Cover the roasting pan tightly with foil and place in the hot oven. Bake the ribs for 3½ hours, or until the meat comes cleanly off the bone. Remove from the oven and leave to cool.

Just before serving, brush the rib racks generously with the blackberry brandy BBQ sauce and grill on a medium-hot griddle or over medium coals until just heated through.

Serve the hot rib racks with Asian slaw and a generous helping of freshly cooked French fries.

INGREDIENTS

1 cup brown sugar

⅓ cup Jamaican jerk seasoning

4½ teaspoons blackened seasoning

2 tablespoons salt

6 racks baby back pork ribs, fat trimmed, about 8–10oz each

1½ cups Coca Cola®

1 cup water

¼ cup liquid smoke

1 tablespoon Worcestershire sauce

1 recipe quantity Blackberry Brandy BBQ Sauce *(see page 126)*

1 recipe quantity Asian Slaw *(see page 143)*

French fries, to serve

CAPTAIN COOK'S BREAD PUDDING

INGREDIENTS

2 tablespoons butter
1lb Granny Smith apples, peeled, cored, quartered, and cut into ¼-inch thick slices
1¼ cups sugar
2 tablespoons golden raisins

SERVES 6

Pre-heat the oven to 350°F. Use half the butter to grease a 9 x 9 x 2-inch baking pan.

Heat the remaining butter in a large skillet over medium heat. Add the apple slices, 4 tablespoons sugar, and the raisins and cook until the apple is tender. Remove from the heat. Carefully add the bourbon, return to the heat and allow to simmer for about 2 minutes, or until all the alcohol is burned off. Set aside.

Place the egg yolks and vanilla extract with 10 tablespoons sugar in a large mixing bowl and beat until the mixture is very thick and "ribbons" or trails of mixture clearly form when the beater is pulled through it. In a saucepan, heat the milk and whipping cream until just boiling. Gradually add the hot cream to the egg-yolk mixture, a little at a time, beating well after each addition to thoroughly incorporate.

In another large mixing bowl, beat the egg whites until they form soft peaks.

Stir the apple mixture into the egg yolk and cream mixture, mixing well. Carefully fold in the bread cubes, until the liquid is absorbed. Gently fold in the beaten egg whites.

Sprinkle the remaining sugar over the sides of the greased baking pan to coat, then tip in the prepared bread-pudding mixture and spread out evenly in the pan. Cover tightly with foil and place in a large roasting pan. Fill the roasting pan with water, so that it comes about half way up the sides of the baking pan of pudding mix. Place in the hot oven for 1½ hours, topping up the water in the roasting pan if it dries out.

To serve, place a piece of warm pudding on each of six serving dishes. Ladle whiskey sauce around the edge of the pudding and drizzle caramel sauce in a zigzag fashion across it. Pipe some sweetened whipped cream in the center of the pudding. Make a small well in the center of the cream and fill with more caramel sauce, then zigzag some caramel sauce over the top of the cream. Dust lightly with powdered sugar and serve.

½ cup bourbon

6 egg yolks

1 teaspoon vanilla extract

1½ cups whole milk

1 cup whipping cream

4 egg whites

12oz sourdough bread, cut into 1-inch cubes

1 recipe quantity Whiskey Sauce *(see page 151)*

1 recipe quantity Caramel Sauce *(see page 150)*

1 recipe quantity Sweetened Whipped Cream *(see page 152)*

powdered sugar, for dusting

BLACKBEARD'S BUTTERSCOTCH

SERVES 6

Take six 16-oz goblets and place about 3 tablespoons of chocolate sauce in each. Tip each goblet so that the chocolate sauce swirls all around the sides to form a thin coating. Chill in the refrigerator until set and ready to serve.

Place the whipping cream, milk, brown sugar, and salt in a large saucepan over medium heat. Bring to the boil, stirring to dissolve the sugar. Allow to boil for about 30 seconds, whisking briskly. Remove from the heat and set aside.

Whip the egg yolks and cornstarch together in a large bowl until they become a pale yellow color. Slowly beat in the warm cream mixture, a cup at a time, stirring until smooth. Pour back into the saucepan and place over medium heat. Allow to simmer, whisking constantly, for 5–7 minutes or until the mixture is very thick and creamy. It is ready when pulling the whisk or beater through it leaves clear trails or "ribbons." Stir in the butter pieces until melted, then stir in the Scotch whiskey and vanilla extract. Remove from the heat. Strain through a wire-mesh strainer and leave to stand for about 30 minutes at room temperature, stirring occasionally.

Divide the pudding mixture between the six chilled, chocolate-lined goblets. Drizzle additional chocolate sauce in a zigzag fashion over the pudding. Pipe sweetened whipped cream up high in the middle of each pudding and drizzle caramel sauce in a zigzag fashion over the cream. Top with chocolate shavings. Stick two pineapple fronds in the top of each serving, like rabbit ears.

INGREDIENTS

1 recipe quantity Chocolate Sauce *(see page 150)*

4 cups whipping cream

2 cups whole milk

1¾ cups dark brown sugar

1 teaspoon salt

6 egg yolks

½ cup cornstarch

8 tablespoons butter, cut into small cubes

4 teaspoons Scotch whiskey

1½ teaspoons vanilla extract

1 recipe quantity Sweetened Whipped Cream *(see page 152)*

1 recipe quantity Caramel Sauce *(see page 150)*

chocolate shavings and 12 fresh pineapple fronds, to decorate

finishing touches

Tommy Bahama®

ASIL OLIVE & WALNUT SAUCE WASABI
UTTER SAUCE ISLAND TARTAR SAUCE
LACKBERRY BRANDY BBQ SAUCE
EMON GARLIC OIL BEER BATTER LIME
OUR CREAM SWEET CHILI MUSTARD
AUCE JERK SAUCE ROASTED RED
EPPER CREAM SAUCE HONEY ROASTED
NIONS ONION STRINGS FRIED
ORTILLA STRIPS WONTON CRISPS
ABY BOK CHOY & SHITAKES BLANCHED
ROCCOLINI ROASTED GARLIC CLOVES
OASTED GARLIC PUREE ROASTED
ARLIC MASHED POTATOES SWEET
HILI GLAZE CILANTRO OIL PORT WINE
EMI-GLACE SAUCE GARLIC AIOLI
ASABI AIOLI MANGO SALSA ASIAN
LAW PASTA SALAD MACADAMIA NUT
RUST HONEY LIME DRESSING LIME
INAIGRETTE LILIKOI VINAIGRETTE
WEET SOY GLAZE TAMARIND
INAIGRETTE BALSAMIC VINAIGRETTE
LUE CHEESE DRESSING CHOCOLATE
AUCE CARAMEL SAUCE WHISKEY
AUCE SWEETENED WHIPPED CREAM
OASTED COCONUT BASIL OLIVE &

BASIL, OLIVE, AND WALNUT SAUCE

INGREDIENTS

½ cup shelled walnuts, lightly toasted

¾ cup fresh basil leaves, roughly chopped

½ cup flat-leaf parsley, roughly chopped and squeezed dry

½ cup freshly grated Parmesan (Grana Padana)

6 anchovy fillets, rinsed, dried, and chopped

1½ tablespoons capers, squeezed dry

½ cup Kalamata olives, pitted and sliced

2 teaspoons coarsely ground black pepper

¼ cup olive oil

Place all the the ingredients in a bowl and fold well together, using a wooden spoon. Cover and keep in the refrigerator or a cool place until needed.

WASABI BUTTER SAUCE

ISLAND TARTAR SAUCE

INGREDIENTS

2 shallots, finely chopped
1 tablespoon wasabi powder
1 cup dry white wine
1 cup mirin (sweet rice wine)
4floz heavy cream
1lb unsalted butter, cut into 1-inch dice
1½ tablespoons light soy sauce

Put the shallots, wasabi powder, white wine, and mirin into a medium saucepan and bring to a gentle boil. Leave to simmer until the liquid is reduced and the mixture has a slushy consistency. Stir in the cream and continue cooking over low heat until the volume is reduced by half.

Move the pan so that it is resting just on the edge of a low flame and stir in the butter, one piece at a time. As soon as one piece begins to melt, add another, continuing until all the butter is melted in.

Remove the pan from the heat and strain the mixture through a fine sieve, pushing down with the back of a spoon on the shallots to release their flavors. Stir in the soy sauce and keep warm until needed.

INGREDIENTS

1 cup mayonnaise
¼ cup pickle relish
1 tablespoon lime juice
pinch cayenne pepper
large pinch onion powder
large pinch garlic powder

Place all the ingredients in a medium mixing bowl and blend together thoroughly using a wooden spoon. Cover and keep in a cool place or the refrigerator until needed.

BLACKBERRY BRANDY BBQ SAUCE

INGREDIENTS

1 cup, plus 2 tablespoons clear honey

1 cup Worcestershire sauce

¾ cup, plus 2 tablespoons tomato ketchup

½ cup blackberry brandy

⅓ cup red wine vinegar

1 small shallot, finely chopped

2 tablespoons cornstarch

2 tablespoons water

Place all the ingredients, except the cornstarch and water, in a large saucepan. Bring to a boil over medium-high heat. Reduce the heat and leave to simmer, uncovered, for 45 minutes. Remove from heat.

Combine the cornstarch and water in a small bowl to form a smooth paste. Stir the cornstarch paste into the hot sauce mixture in the pan. Place the pan over low heat and cook gently, stirring, until the sauce is thick enough to coat the back of a spoon. Cover and keep until needed.

LEMON GARLIC OIL

BEER BATTER

INGREDIENTS

3 cups olive oil	
1 cup freshly squeezed lemon juice	
1 recipe quantity Roasted Garlic Purée *(see page 135)*	
2 teaspoons salt	
1 teaspoon coarsely ground black pepper	

Place all the ingredients in a large mixing bowl and whisk well until thoroughly blended. Keep covered in a refrigerator or cool place and use as needed.

INGREDIENTS

10oz packet seafood batter mix	
4 teaspoons dried thyme	
2 tablespoons coarsely ground black pepper	
1 tablespoon salt	
2 cups beer	

Place the batter mix, dried thyme, pepper, and salt in a large mixing bowl and combine until well mixed. Gradually whisk in the beer to form a batter. Keep covered in a cool place until needed.

127

LIME SOUR CREAM

SWEET CHILI MUSTARD SAUCE

INGREDIENTS

¾ cup sour cream

1 tablespoon fresh lime juice

Place the ingredients in a small bowl and whisk together until well blended. Cover and keep in the refrigerator until needed.

INGREDIENTS

1 cup Asian sweet chili sauce

2 tablespoons wholegrain mustard

2 tablespoons soy sauce

1 tablespoon rice vinegar

Place all the ingredients in a medium bowl and whisk together until well combined. Cover and keep until needed.

JERK SAUCE

INGREDIENTS

1 cup A.1.® steak sauce

¾ cup mayonnaise

2 tablespoons Worcestershire sauce

1 tablespoon fresh lemon juice

1 tablespoon Tabasco® sauce

2 teaspoons Jamaican jerk seasoning

2 teaspoons paprika

3 cloves garlic, finely chopped

1½ teaspoons balsamic vinegar

½ teaspoon sugar

½ teaspoon finely ground black pepper

¼ teaspoon cayenne pepper

pinch crushed dried red chili pepper

Place all the ingredients in a medium mixing bowl and whisk together until well combined. Cover and keep in a cool place until needed.

ROASTED RED PEPPER CREAM SAUCE

INGREDIENTS

3 medium red bell peppers, halved lengthways and deseeded

1 tablespoon olive oil

1 recipe quantity Roasted Garlic Purée *(see page 135)*

2 medium shallots, finely chopped

pinch dried thyme

2 tablespoons dry sherry

1 cup chicken stock

1 cup whipping cream

1 tablespoon butter

1 tablespoon all-purpose flour

salt

freshly ground black pepper

Pre-heat the oven to 400°F. Place the pepper halves, skin-side-up, in a roasting pan and cook in hot oven until the skin is blackened and blistered. Remove from the oven. Scrape off the blackened skin with a sharp knife and discard. Chop up the remaining flesh and set aside.

Heat the olive oil in a medium saucepan. Add the roasted red pepper, roasted garlic purée, shallots, and dried thyme and cook over medium heat for 5 minutes, or until the shallots have softened. Remove from heat. Stir in the sherry, return to heat and cook for 1 minute, stirring to remove any browned bits from the bottom of the pan.

Pour in the chicken stock and whipping cream and bring to a boil.

Meanwhile, melt the butter in a small saucepan. Remove from heat, stir in the flour until well blended and cook over low heat for 1–2 minutes. Whisk into the just boiling sauce until thoroughly combined. Reduce the heat and leave to simmer gently for 6–8 minutes, or until the sauce is slightly thickened.

Season to taste with salt and pepper and allow to cool slightly. Pour into a blender or food processor and blend until smooth. Cover and keep warm until needed.

HONEY ROASTED ONIONS

ONION STRINGS

INGREDIENTS

1 tablespoon olive oil

1½lb yellow onions, thinly sliced

2 tablespoons clear honey

1 tablespoon molasses

large pinch salt

pinch freshly ground black pepper

pinch crushed dried red chili pepper

Heat the olive oil in a large skillet over medium heat. Add all the remaining ingredients and cook, stirring, until the onions are soft and translucent. Set aside and keep warm until needed.

INGREDIENTS

1 large Vidalia or other sweet onion

¾ cup all-purpose flour

1½ teaspoons sugar

1½ teaspoons salt

sunflower or peanut oil for deep-frying

salt and freshly ground pepper, to season

Peel and thinly slice the onion. Place the sliced onion in a bowl of ice water and leave for 5–10 minutes. Meanwhile, combine the flour, sugar, and salt in a large mixing bowl and set aside.

Heat the oil in a deep pan until hot enough to brown a small cube of bread in about 30 seconds. Drain the onion well. Add a few slices at a time to the flour mixture, tossing to coat well. Shake off any excess flour and cook in small batches in the hot oil for 30–45 seconds, or until golden brown. Drain on paper towels and season to taste with salt and pepper. Serve hot.

131

FRIED TORTILLA STRIPS

INGREDIENTS

sunflower or peanut oil for deep-frying

2 large corn tortillas, cut into 3 x ⅛-inch strips

1 teaspoon ground cumin

½ teaspoon cayenne pepper

Heat the oil in a deep pan until hot enough to brown a small cube of bread in about 30 seconds.

Add the corn tortilla strips and cook for 1–2 minutes until crisp and golden. Remove from the pan and drain well on paper towels.

Sprinkle with the cumin and cayenne pepper and use immediately.

WONTON CRISPS

INGREDIENTS

sunflower or peanut oil for deep-frying

12 wonton wrappers, cut into 3 x 3 inch squares

Heat the oil in a deep pan until hot enough to brown a small cube of bread in about 30 seconds.

Add the wonton wrapper squares to the hot oil and cook for 1–2 minutes until crisp and golden. Remove from the pan and drain well on paper towels.

BABY BOK CHOY AND SHITAKES

INGREDIENTS

salt
1½lb baby bok choy
1 tablespoon peanut oil
12oz shitake mushrooms, stems removed and halved
freshly ground black pepper

Bring a large saucepan of water to a boil. Add a pinch of salt and the baby bok choy and cook for 2–3 minutes, until just starting to become tender. Drain and transfer the bok choy to a bowl of ice water to chill and stop any further cooking. Drain again and cut into quarters lengthwise. Set aside.

Heat the oil in a large skillet. Add the prepared bok choy and the shitake mushrooms and cook over medium heat until tender and the mushrooms are lightly browned. Serve hot, seasoned to taste with salt and pepper.

133

BLANCHED BROCCOLINI

INGREDIENTS

salt

1lb broccolini, cut into 4-inch long florets

Bring a large saucepan of water to a boil. Add a pinch of salt and the broccolini florets. Cook over medium heat for 3–4 minutes, then drain. Transfer the broccolini to a bowl of ice water to chill and stop any further cooking. Drain again and set aside until needed.

Just before serving, reheat the broccolini by sautéing gently in a large skillet for 3–4 minutes. Serve hot.

ROASTED GARLIC CLOVES

ROASTED GARLIC PURÉE

INGREDIENTS

1 large bulb fresh garlic

1 tablespoon olive oil

Pre-heat the oven to 350°F.

Place the whole garlic bulb on a piece of aluminum foil on a baking sheet. Drizzle with the olive oil, then fold up the foil around the garlic to seal it in.

Place the garlic in the hot oven and roast for 45 minutes, or until the cloves are soft. Remove from the oven, break up the garlic and use the individual cloves as a garnish, with or without their skins.

INGREDIENTS

2 large bulbs garlic

⅓ cup olive oil

Pre-heat the oven to 350°F. Divide the garlic up into cloves. Peel the cloves, discarding the papery outer skins.

Place the peeled cloves in a medium-sized baking dish and pour on the olive oil. Bake in the hot oven for 40 minutes, or until the garlic is light brown. Remove from the oven and leave to cool for 30 minutes.

Transfer the cooled garlic cloves to a blender or food processor and blend until smooth and creamy. Cover and keep in a cool place until required.

ROASTED GARLIC MASHED POTATOES

INGREDIENTS

1¼lb russet potatoes

salt

⅓ cup whipping cream

3oz butter

2 tablespoons Roasted Garlic Purée *(see page 135)*

freshly ground black pepper

Wash and peel the potatoes. Cut in half and place in a large saucepan with enough water to cover. Bring to a boil, add a pinch of salt, reduce the heat and leave to simmer for 20–25 minutes, or until tender. Drain.

Return the drained potatoes to a clean saucepan and use a potato masher to mash coarsely. Stir in the whipping cream, butter and roasted garlic purée, until well blended. Season to taste with salt and pepper. Heat through gently over low-medium heat and serve.

SWEET CHILI GLAZE

CILANTRO OIL

INGREDIENTS

1 cup Asian sweet chili sauce

2 tablespoons sesame oil

2 tablespoons rice vinegar

2 tablespoons soy sauce

1 teaspoon ground ginger

Place all the ingredients in a medium mixing bowl. Whisk together until thoroughly blended. Cover and keep in a cool place until needed.

INGREDIENTS

large bunch of fresh cilantro leaves

¾ cup canola oil

Fill a medium saucepan with water and bring to a boil. Lower the heat a little and toss in the cilantro leaves. Allow to cook for about 10 seconds, then drain and quickly transfer the leaves to a bowl of ice water to chill for 5–10 minutes.

Place the chilled cilantro leaves in a blender or food processor. Add the oil and process for 2 minutes. Strain the mixture through a cheesecloth or very fine strainer. Keep the oil in a covered container until required.

PORT WINE DEMI-GLACE SAUCE

INGREDIENTS

1 tablespoon olive oil

3 medium shallots, finely chopped

3–4 sprigs fresh thyme, finely chopped

1 bay leaf

⅓ cup dry red wine

⅓ cup port

½ cup beef stock

1 teaspoon Roasted Garlic Purée *(see page 135)*

salt

freshly ground white pepper

Heat the olive oil in a medium saucepan over medium heat. Add the shallots and cook until lightly golden. Stir in the thyme and bay leaf and cook for another minute. Pour in the red wine and port and bring to a boil, scraping any browned bits from the bottom of the pan. Reduce the heat and leave to simmer, uncovered, until the mixture is reduced by about two-thirds of its original volume. Add the beef stock and return to a boil, then lower the heat again and simmer very gently, uncovered, for 50 minutes. Stir in the roasted garlic purée and a pinch of salt and white pepper. Simmer for 1 minute more, then strain through a fine-mesh strainer. Set aside and keep warm until required.

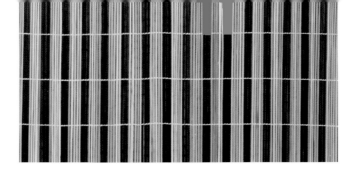

GARLIC AIOLI

WASABI AIOLI

INGREDIENTS

¾ cup 1-inch baguette cubes, crusts removed
3 tablespoons whole milk
4½ teaspoons frozen or chilled liquid egg product
4 cloves garlic, finely chopped
1½ teaspoons Dijon mustard
1½ teaspoons fresh lemon juice
1½ teaspoons red-wine vinegar
large pinch salt
½ cup olive oil

Place the baguette cubes and milk in a small bowl and leave to soak for 15 minutes. Squeeze the liquid from the bread into a blender or food processor, discarding the bread.

Add the egg product, garlic, mustard, lemon juice, red-wine vinegar, and salt to the liquid in the blender. Process for about 30 seconds to incorporate all the ingredients well. With the motor still running, slowly add the olive oil in a thin, steady stream until the oil is well incorporated and the mixture has thickened. Cover and set aside in a cool place or the refrigerator until needed.

INGREDIENTS

½ cup Garlic Aioli *(see left)*
1½ teaspoons wasabi powder
1½ teaspoons water

Place the garlic aioli in a small bowl. Stir in the wasabi powder and water until well blended. Cover and set aside in a cool place until needed.

MANGO SALSA

INGREDIENTS

4 medium fresh mangoes

½ jalapeño pepper, deseeded and finely chopped

3 green onions, trimmed and sliced diagonally

1 large red bell pepper, deseeded and finely chopped

1 tablespoon fresh lime juice

1 tablespoon olive oil

1 teaspoon finely chopped fresh cilantro

large pinch salt

pinch freshly ground black pepper

Peel and halve the mangoes. Remove and discard the stones, then roughly chop the flesh. Place in a medium mixing bowl with the remaining ingredients. Stir until the ingredients are evenly mixed. Cover and keep in a cool place until needed.

ASIAN SLAW

INGREDIENTS

1 large red onion, peeled and cut into very thin wedges

8oz green cabbage, shredded

3 jicama, peeled and cut into matchsticks

1 tablespoon finely chopped cilantro

½ cup olive oil

4 tablespoons fresh lime juice

large pinch salt

large pinch freshly ground black pepper

Place the onion wedges in a bowl of ice water and leave to stand for 20 minutes. Drain and tip into a medium mixing bowl.

Stir in the cabbage, jicama, and cilantro and mix evenly. Add the olive oil and lime juice and salt and pepper to taste. Toss to coat the salad well. Cover and keep in a cool place until needed.

PASTA SALAD

INGREDIENTS

12oz pennetti pasta

4 medium Roma tomatoes, peeled, seeded, and finely chopped

¼ cup oil-packed, sun-dried tomatoes, roughly chopped

3 medium shallots, finely chopped

¼ cup olive oil

3 tablespoons capers

1 tablespoon chopped fresh parsley

1 tablespoon chopped fresh basil leaves

1 tablespoon balsamic vinegar

large pinch salt

large pinch freshly ground black pepper

1oz *queso fresco*, crumbled

Cook the pasta according to the package directions. Drain and rinse with cold water to chill and stop any further cooking. Drain again and set aside.

In a medium mixing bowl, combine the Roma tomatoes, sun-dried tomatoes, shallots, olive oil, capers, parsley, basil, balsamic vinegar, salt, and pepper until evenly mixed. Gently mix in the cooked, chilled pasta and the queso fresco. Cover and keep in a cool place until needed.

MACADAMIA NUT CRUST

INGREDIENTS

½ cup macadamia nuts

¾ cups panko (Japanese-style) breadcrumbs

1 teaspoon red Hawaiian salt

Pre-heat the oven to 400°F.

Place the nuts in a shallow baking pan and toast in the hot oven for 5–6 minutes, or until beginning to brown. Remove from the oven and leave to cool.

Place the cooled nuts in a blender or food processor and process until finely chopped. Tip into a shallow dish and stir in the panko crumbs and red Hawaiian salt until the ingredients are evenly mixed. Cover and set aside until needed.

HONEY LIME DRESSING

LIME VINAIGRETTE

INGREDIENTS

½ cup fresh lime juice

5 tablespoons clear honey

4½ teaspoons sesame oil

1 tablespoon coarsely chopped cilantro

1 red bell pepper, deseeded and very finely chopped

2½ teaspoons cider vinegar

2½ teaspoons spicy brown mustard

½ teaspoon grated fresh ginger

large pinch salt

pinch coarsely ground black pepper

½ cup olive oil

Place all the ingredients, except the olive oil, in a small bowl and stir to mix evenly. Pour in the olive oil in a slow steady stream, whisking constantly, until all the oil is well incorporated. Cover and set aside in the refrigerator or a cool place until needed.

INGREDIENTS

¼ cup fresh lime juice

½ teaspoon salt

½ teaspoon freshly ground black pepper

½ cup olive oil

Pour the lime juice into a small bowl. Add the salt and pepper and stir until the salt has dissolved. Add the olive oil in a slow steady stream, whisking constantly, until well incorporated. Cover and set aside in a cool place until needed.

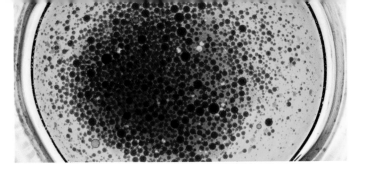

LILIOKI VINAIGRETTE

INGREDIENTS

4½ teaspoons rice vinegar

2 teaspoons clear honey

2 teaspoons passion fruit purée, or frozen passion fruit concentrate

1 teaspoon fresh lime juice

1 clove garlic, finely chopped

¼ teaspoon grated fresh ginger

¼ teaspoon sugar

¼ teaspoon salt

pinch freshly ground black pepper

⅓ cup canola oil

Place all the ingredients, except the canola oil, in a small bowl and whisk until well mixed. Add the oil in a slow, steady stream, whisking constantly, until well incorporated. Cover and set aside in a cool place until needed.

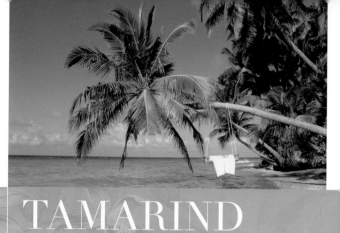

SWEET SOY GLAZE

TAMARIND VINAIGRETTE

INGREDIENTS

2 cups soy sauce

1 cup sugar

1 jalapeño pepper, deseeded and sliced

¾ teaspoon sesame oil

Place the soy sauce, sugar, and jalapeño pepper in a medium saucepan. Bring to a boil, stirring to dissolve the sugar.

Reduce the heat and leave to simmer, uncovered, until the mixture thickens and coats the back of a spoon.

Stir in the sesame oil. Strain through a fine mesh strainer, cover and set aside until needed.

INGREDIENTS

2 tablespoons Asian sweet chili sauce

2 tablespoons rice vinegar

1 tablespoon tamarind paste

2 teaspoons light brown sugar

2 teaspoons soy sauce

¼ teaspoon salt

pinch coarsely ground black pepper

3 tablespoons olive oil

½ teaspoon sesame oil

½ teaspoon black sesame seeds

Place all the ingredients, except the olive oil, sesame oil, and sesame seeds, in a small bowl and whisk together until well mixed.

Add the olive oil, sesame oil, and sesame seeds and whisk well until all the oil is incorporated. Cover and set aside in a cool place until needed.

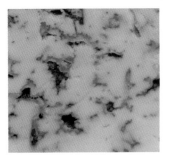

BALSAMIC VINAIGRETTE

BLUE CHEESE DRESSING

INGREDIENTS

2 tablespoons balsamic vinegar

1 teaspoon Dijon mustard

1 teaspoon finely chopped fresh basil leaves

½ teaspoon finely chopped fresh parsley

¼ teaspoon dried oregano

1 clove garlic, finely chopped

¼ teaspoon salt

¼ teaspoon freshly ground black pepper

⅓ cup olive oil

Place all the ingredients, except the olive oil, in a medium mixing bowl and whisk until well mixed.

Pour in the olive oil in a slow, steady stream, whisking constantly, until incorporated. Cover and set aside in a cool place until needed.

INGREDIENTS

⅔ cup mayonnaise

¼ cup sour cream

¼ cup buttermilk

1 teaspoon cider vinegar

pinch coarsely ground black pepper

2oz Maytag® blue cheese, crumbled

Place all the ingredients, except the cheese, in a blender or food processor and process until smooth and well blended.

Transfer to a bowl and stir in the crumbled cheese. Cover and set aside in a cool place until needed.

CHOCOLATE SAUCE

CARAMEL SAUCE

INGREDIENTS

4oz bittersweet chocolate, chopped into small pieces

½ cup whipping cream

1oz butter

1 tablespoon sugar

1 tablespoon Kahlua®

¼ teaspoon vanilla extract

Place the chocolate pieces in a medium bowl and set aside.

Place the whipping cream, butter, sugar, and Kahlua in a medium saucepan. Cook over medium heat, stirring constantly, until the sugar has dissolved.

Remove from the heat and pour over the chocolate in the bowl. Add the vanilla extract and gently fold the cream mixture into the chocolate using a rubber spatula, mixing until the chocolate is melted. Whisk until smooth and well incorporated. Cover and set aside until needed.

INGREDIENTS

1¾ cups sugar

4oz butter

⅔ cup whipping cream

Place the sugar and butter in a medium saucepan over medium heat, stirring constantly until the sugar dissolves and then frequently, until the mixture is a deep caramel color.

Reduce the heat to very low and slowly and carefully pour in the whipping cream, whisking constantly to incorporate. Leave to simmer for 1 minute. Strain through a fine mesh strainer. Leave to cool at room temperature. Cover and set aside until needed.

WHISKEY SAUCE

INGREDIENTS

¼ cup whipping cream

3 tablespoons sugar

1 teaspoon butter

pinch ground cinnamon

1 tablespoon bourbon

¼ teaspoon cornstarch

Place the whipping cream, sugar, butter, and cinnamon in a small saucepan over medium heat and stir constantly until the sugar dissolves. Remove from the heat and set aside.

Mix the bourbon and cornstarch together in a small bowl until well blended. Stir into the cream mixture in the pan and return to the heat. Cook for 2 minutes or until slightly thickened, stirring constantly.

Pour the sauce into a mixing bowl and place in another bowl filled with enough ice to come halfway up the sides of the bowl of sauce. Stir occasionally to cool and thicken.

Cover and set aside until needed.

SWEETENED WHIPPED CREAM

INGREDIENTS

4 cups whipping cream

⅓ cup powdered sugar

1 teaspoon vanilla extract

Place all the ingredients in a large mixing bowl. Whisk until the mixture forms stiff peaks.

Cover and set aside in a cool place until needed.

TOASTED COCONUT

INGREDIENTS

2 tablespoons shredded coconut

½ tablespoon powdered sugar

Pre-heat the oven to 300°F.

Place the ingredients in a medium bowl and mix together well. Spread the mixture evenly in a thin layer over a baking sheet. Place in the hot oven and cook for 10–15 minutes, or until the coconut is mostly a golden brown. Stir about every 4 minutes so that the coconut browns evenly.

one sip at a time

Tommy Bahama®

HAVANA SUN TOMMY'S CLASSIC
DAIQUIRI TOMMY COLLINS BAHAMA
BASIL SMASH TOMMY'S CLASSIC
MOJITO GOLDEN SUN & GINGER
BARBADOS COBBLER MAI-TOMMY
TOMMY MAI-TAI PEACHY KEEN
TOMMY ZOMBIE BLUE HAWAIIAN
BOMA-BAHAMA POLYNESIAN
PARADISE CRAZY CUBAN TOMMY'S
TROPICAL MOMENT HURRICANE
TOMMY TOMMY APPLE PIE
MARTINI GOLDEN SUN EGG NOG
AFTER DARK WHITE SAND TOAST
PEPPERMINT MARTINI GOLDEN SUN
PUMPKIN PIE NUTTY SUN GOLDEN
APPLE MILLIONAIRE MOJITO
COSMOPOLITAN TOMMY-TINI TOMMY
BAHAMA BAY BREEZE WHITE SAND
CUBA LIBRE BAHAMA SUNRISE
KEY LIME MARTINI VELVET ROSA
BAILEY'S BANANA COLADA CANT-E-
LOPE TONIGHT COCONUT CLOUD
MARTINI HAV-AN-A KEY LIME BRONX

THE RUM STORY

Tommy Bahama

Ultra Premium Rum
Handcrafted on
the Island of Barbados
Taste Paradise…One Sip at a Time

Tommy Bahama rum is crafted on the beautiful island of Barbados—the most easterly of all the Caribbean islands, where the combination of year-round, warm temperatures and cooling trade winds creates the perfect environment for rum-making.

Only the purest, clearest water—naturally filtered through coral stone—and the finest blackstrap molasses are used in Tommy Bahama rums. No sugar or artificial blender is added. They are created at R. L. Seale's legendary Foursquare Distillery, which has been making award-winning rums for more than 80 years. Aged slowly in small batches for a minimum of 2 years in American, white oak barrels, then blended to perfection by a master distiller, the result is rum of truly sublime elegance.

Tommy Bahama offers rum in two delightfully distinct flavors. White Sand®, a clear, light-bodied rum, is aged for a minimum of 2 years. It has a smooth entry and a clean, tangy finish, with hints of tropical fruit. Golden Sun®, a full-bodied amber rum, is aged for up to 10 years to produce a fruity nose and a taste nuanced with hints of coffee, roasted nuts, and sweet pralines. Both Tommy Bahama rums are versatile enough to be mixed in cocktails, yet complex and mature enough to be sipped neat, or on the rocks.

Barbados

B arbados is the birthplace of rum. It is no accident that many of the world's finest rums are made on this small island, where sugar cane grows readily, thanks to a climate of almost endless sunshine and gently cooling trade winds. The island's rums are noted for their smoothness and depth of flavor—and Tommy Bahama® rums are no exception.

A LITTLE HISTORY

The ancient Chinese are said to have made an alcoholic drink from sugar-cane juice, and the explorer Marco Polo (c.1254–1324) records being offered such a beverage on his travels in the Far East. The fermentation of molasses to make alcohol began on Caribbean sugar plantations in the 17th century. As the drink's popularity spread to North America and Europe,

MAKING RUM

Fermentation The story of rum starts with the sugar-cane harvest in early autumn. Blackstrap molasses—made by boiling sugar-cane syrup—is blended with water and carefully selected yeasts, and then left to ferment very slowly in large metal vats.

Distillation The alcoholic liquid, produced by fermentation, is placed in a still, where it is heated until the alcohol in it vaporizes. This vapor passes through a series of pipes, where it cools and condenses, creating a liquid with a high alcohol content—basic rum.

Ageing & Blending The basic rum now needs time to mature, for varying lengths of time depending on the style, to develop character and depth of flavor. Finally, samples from different batches of aged rum are blended by a master of the craft. The result is a spirit of unparalleled quality.

to give daily rations of watered-down rum (called "grog") to its sailors, and it became renowned as the drink of choice for pirates.

Rum, aged in oak barrels, prepared for blending

RUM STYLES

Dark rum is a rich, heavy spirit with a distinct, smoky flavor that comes from being left to mature slowly in charred barrels. Amber rums, such as Tommy Bahama's Golden Sun®, are medium-bodied with a radiant, gold color. Spiced rums are usually amber rums flavored with exotic spices, while light and white rums, such as Tommy Bahama's White Sand®, make excellent mixers for cocktails. These rums are aged in uncharred oak barrels and distilled using a continuous process to create a clean, neutral spirit.

Harvesting sugar cane, Barbados

MASTER DISTILLERS

Tommy Bahama's rums are made at the Foursquare Distillery, near St. Philip, Barbados, which has been in operation for four generations. The skill and experience of these master distillers is reflected in every bottle. All of their award-winning rums are fermented using only the best, all-natural ingredients in small batches and blended individually by hand. This ensures that the subtle character differences found in each batch of matured rum are always perfectly matched. The result is a taste of paradise.

Blending tanks, Foursquare Distillery, Barbados

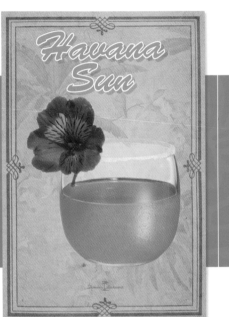

Havana Sun

INGREDIENTS

1 tablespoon sugar

1½oz Tommy Bahama Golden Sun® rum

½oz triple sec

½oz freshly squeezed lime juice

½oz simple (sugar) syrup

orange juice

orange bitters

Sprinkle the sugar over a small plate. Wet the rim of a chilled lowball glass, then dip it in the sugar to coat it.

Pour the rum, triple sec, lime juice, and syrup into a chilled cocktail shaker. Splash in a little orange juice, then add a dash of orange bitters. Top with a few scoops of crushed ice. Shake until the mixture is well blended and thoroughly chilled.

Strain into the prepared sugar-rimmed glass. Garnish with an edible flower and serve.

INGREDIENTS

2oz Tommy Bahama White Sand® rum

1oz freshly squeezed lime juice

½oz simple (sugar) syrup

Place all the ingredients in a chilled cocktail shaker. Add a few scoops of crushed ice, according to taste.

Shake until the mixture is icy cold and well blended.

Pour into a chilled cocktail glass. Garnish with a twist of fresh lime peel and serve.

Tommy Collins

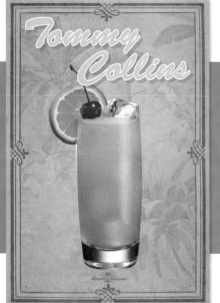

INGREDIENTS

2oz Tommy Bahama White Sand® rum

1oz freshly squeezed lemon juice

1 teaspoon simple (sugar) syrup or superfine sugar

club soda

Pour the rum and lemon juice into a chilled cocktail shaker. Stir in the simple syrup or superfine sugar.

Add some crushed ice, according to taste, and shake until the mixture is thoroughly chilled and blended.

Pour into a chilled highball glass. Top with club soda to fill the glass. Garnish with a slice of fresh orange and a maraschino cherry, and serve.

INGREDIENTS

4 fresh blackberries

4 fresh basil leaves

4 fresh ginger slices

2oz Tommy Bahama White Sand® rum

½oz freshly squeezed lemon juice

¾oz simple (sugar) syrup

club soda

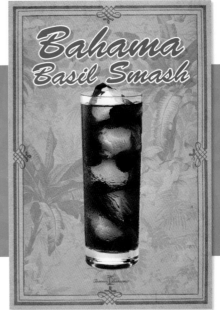

Bahama
Basil Smash

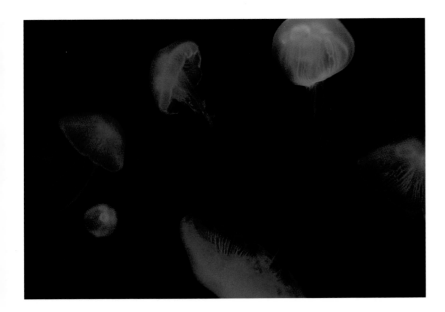

Place the blackberries, basil leaves, and ginger in a chilled cocktail shaker. Stir to mix, breaking up the blackberries and basil slightly.

Stir in the rum, lemon juice, and syrup. Add some ice, to taste, and shake well until the mixture is thoroughly chilled and blended.

Strain into a chilled highball glass. Add fresh ice, to taste, and top with a splash of club soda. Serve, garnished with whole blackberries.

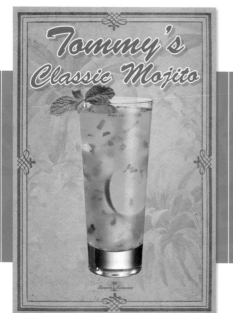

Tommy's Classic Mojito

INGREDIENTS

2oz Tommy Bahama White Sand® rum

1 teaspoon superfine sugar

1oz freshly squeezed lime juice

handful of fresh mint leaves, roughly chopped

club soda

Place the rum, sugar, lime juice, and mint leaves in a chilled cocktail shaker. Stir to mix.

Add several scoops of crushed ice, to taste, and shake until the mixture is icy cold and well blended.

Pour into a tall, chilled glass. Add club soda to top off the glass. Serve, garnished with a mint sprig and a slice of fresh lime.

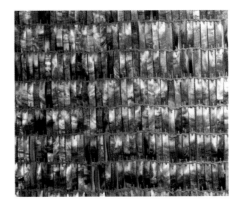

INGREDIENTS

2oz Tommy Bahama Golden Sun® rum

ginger ale

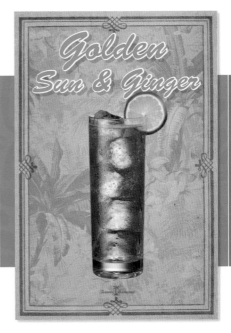

Golden
Sun & Ginger

ONE SIP AT A TIME

Fill a tall glass with ice cubes. Pour in the rum, then top off the glass with enough ginger ale to fill.

Stir gently. Serve garnished with a slice of fresh lime.

Barbados Cobbler

INGREDIENTS

2oz Tommy Bahama Golden Sun® rum

¼oz crème de cacao

½oz freshly squeezed lime juice

½oz simple (sugar) syrup

3oz pineapple juice

pinch of powdered cinnamon

Angostura® bitters

Pour the rum, crème de cacao, lime juice, syrup, and pineapple juice into a chilled cocktail shaker. Stir in the cinnamon, then add a couple of dashes of Angostura bitters.

Add some crushed ice, to taste, and shake well until the mixture is thoroughly chilled and well blended.

Strain into a tall glass, partly filled with fresh ice. Serve, garnished with a sprinkling of grated nutmeg and a sprig of fresh mint.

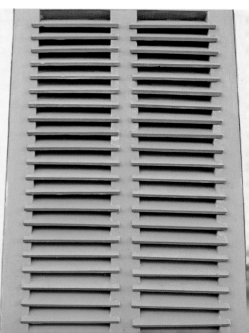

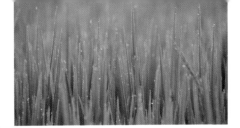

INGREDIENTS

1oz Tommy Bahama White Sand® rum

1oz Tommy Bahama Golden Sun® rum

½oz coconut rum

2oz orange juice

2oz pineapple juice

grenadine syrup

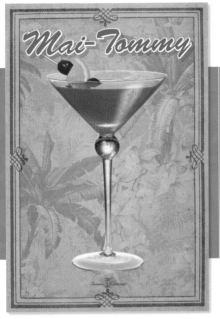

Place the rums, orange juice, and pineapple juice in a chilled cocktail shaker. Add a few splashes of grenadine syrup and several scoops of crushed ice, according to taste.

Shake well until the mixture is thoroughly blended and icy cold.

Strain into a chilled martini glass. Serve, garnished with a slice of fresh orange and a couple of maraschino cherries.

Tommy Mai-Tai

INGREDIENTS

¾oz Tommy Bahama Golden Sun® rum

¾oz Tommy Bahama White Sand® rum

½oz almond-flavored liqueur

½oz triple sec

½oz orange juice

½oz pineapple juice

grenadine syrup

Pour the rums, almond liqueur, and triple sec into a chilled cocktail shaker. Add a few scoops of crushed ice, according to taste.

Shake until the mixture is well blended and thoroughly chilled.

Pour into a chilled hurricane or highball glass, half-filled with fresh ice. Stir in the orange and pineapple juices, then float a little grenadine syrup on the top. Serve, garnished with a maraschino cherry and a fresh pineapple slice.

INGREDIENTS

1oz Tommy Bahama Golden Sun® rum

1½oz peach schnapps

½oz passion fruit juice

1oz mango juice

1oz freshly squeezed orange juice

Peachy Keen

Place all the ingredients in a chilled cocktail shaker. Stir in a few scoops of crushed ice, according to taste.

Shake well until the mixture is thoroughly mixed and chilled.

Strain into a chilled martini glass. Serve, garnished with an orchid on the rim of the glass.

Tommy Zombie

INGREDIENTS

1oz Tommy Bahama White Sand® rum	
1oz Tommy Bahama Golden Sun® rum	
⅓oz each cherry brandy and apricot brandy	
⅓oz freshly squeezed lime juice	
2oz pineapple juice	
1oz orange juice	
orgeat (almond) syrup	

Pour both rums, together with the cherry and apricot brandies, into a chilled cocktail shaker. Stir in the lime juice, pineapple juice, orange juice, and a dash of orgeat syrup. Top off with a few scoops of crushed ice, according to taste.

Shake until the mixture is well blended and thoroughly chilled.

Pour into a chilled tiki-style cup. Serve, garnished with slices of fresh orange or lime and a sprig of mint.

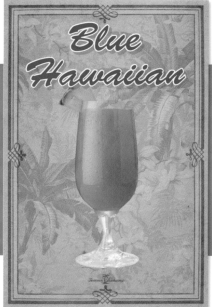

Blue Hawaiian

INGREDIENTS

1oz Tommy Bahama White Sand® rum

1oz blue curaçao

1oz coconut cream

2oz pineapple juice

Pour all the ingredients into a chilled blender. Add a couple of scoops of crushed ice, according to taste.

Process until the mixture is thoroughly blended and smooth.

Pour into a chilled hurricane glass. Serve, garnished with a wedge of fresh pineapple.

171

Poma-Bahama

INGREDIENTS

2oz Tommy Bahama White Sand® rum

1oz pomegranate liqueur

splash of cranberry juice

splash of freshly squeezed lime juice

Put all the ingredients into a chilled cocktail shaker. Add a few scoops of crushed ice, according to taste.

Shake well until the mixture is well blended and thoroughly chilled.

Strain into a chilled martini glass. Serve, garnished with a twist of fresh orange or lime peel.

INGREDIENTS

2oz Tommy Bahama Golden Sun® rum

4oz pineapple juice

1oz orange juice

1oz coconut cream

freshly grated nutmeg

Polynesian Paradise

Pour all the ingredients, except the nutmeg, into a chilled cocktail shaker. Top off with a couple of scoops of crushed ice.

Shake well until the mixture is thoroughly mixed and well chilled.

Pour into a lowball glass. Sprinkle a little freshly grated nutmeg over the top. Serve, garnished with a wedge of fresh orange.

Crazy Cuban

INGREDIENTS

1oz Tommy Bahama White Sand® rum

½oz Tommy Bahama Golden Sun® rum

1oz coconut rum

½oz banana schnapps

3oz pineapple juice

Pour all the ingredients into a tall, chilled glass. Add a scoop or two of crushed ice and stir to mix well.

Serve, garnished with a wedge of fresh pineapple, a maraschino cherry, and a paper parasol.

INGREDIENTS

1oz Tommy Bahama White Sand® rum

½oz orange juice

½oz pineapple juice

¼oz piña colada mix

grenadine syrup

1oz Tommy Bahama Golden Sun® rum

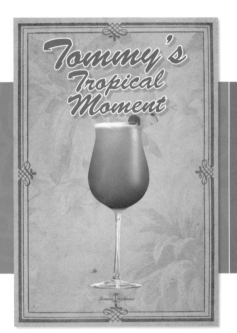

Tommy's Tropical Moment

Place the White Sand rum, orange juice, pineapple juice, piña colada mix, and a dash of grenadine syrup in a chilled cocktail shaker.

Add a couple of scoops of crushed ice and shake until well mixed and chilled.

Strain into a hurricane glass, add a scoop of fresh ice, and top off with the Golden Sun rum. Serve, garnished with a maraschino cherry and a wedge of fresh pineapple.

Hurricane Tommy

INGREDIENTS

1½oz Tommy Bahama Golden Sun® rum
1½oz Tommy Bahama White Sand® rum
2oz passion fruit juice
1½oz orange juice
1½oz pineapple juice
½oz freshly squeezed lime juice

Pour all the ingredients into a chilled cocktail shaker. Shake to mix well.

Place a few scoops of crushed ice in a chilled hurricane glass, then pour in the mixed cocktail.

Stir and serve, garnished with a wedge of fresh pineapple and a couple of maraschino cherries.

INGREDIENTS

1 tablespoon fine graham cracker crumbs

1½oz Tommy Bahama White Sand® rum

½oz sour apple schnapps

¼ teaspoon half and half

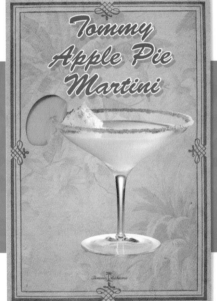

Tommy Apple Pie Martini

Spread the graham cracker crumbs on a small plate. Wet the rim of a chilled cocktail glass, then dip it into the cracker crumbs to coat the rim well.

Pour the rum, sour apple schnapps, and half and half into a chilled cocktail shaker. Add a scoop or two of crushed ice and shake to mix well. Tip into the prepared crumb-rimmed glass.

Serve, garnished with a spoonful of whipped cream, a slice of fresh apple, and a sprinkling of freshly grated nutmeg or powdered cinnamon.

Golden Sun Egg Nog

INGREDIENTS

2oz Tommy Bahama White Sand® rum

4oz egg nog

freshly grated nutmeg

Pour the rum and egg nog into a chilled cocktail shaker. Add one or two scoops of crushed ice, according to taste. Shake until the mixture is well blended and thoroughly chilled through.

Strain into a chilled glass cup and sprinkle over a little freshly grated nutmeg. Serve, garnished with a stick of cinnamon.

After Dark

INGREDIENTS

2oz Tommy Bahama Golden Sun® rum

1oz orange liqueur

1oz freshly prepared espresso coffee, chilled

½oz simple (sugar) syrup

freshly grated nutmeg

cocoa powder

Place all the ingredients, except the cocoa powder, in a chilled cocktail shaker. Add a few scoops of crushed ice, according to taste.

Shake until the mixture is thoroughly blended and icy cold.

Pour into a chilled martini glass. Lightly sprinkle a little cocoa powder over the top and serve.

181

White Sand Toast

INGREDIENTS

2oz Tommy Bahama White Sand® rum

2oz cranberry juice

Champagne

Pour the rum and cranberry juice into a chilled cocktail shaker.

Add a scoop or two of crushed ice, according to taste, and shake well until the mixture is thoroughly chilled through and well blended.

Strain into a chilled champagne flute. Carefully pour Champagne into the glass to fill. Serve, garnished with a fresh cranberry.

INGREDIENTS

1 tablespoon dark chocolate shavings

1½oz Tommy Bahama White Sand® rum

1oz peppermint schnapps

1oz crème de cacao

1oz light cream

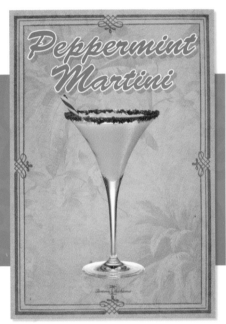

Peppermint Martini

Spread the chocolate shavings out on a small plate. Wet the rim of a chilled cocktail glass, then dip it into the chocolate until the rim is well coated.

Place the remaining ingredients in a chilled cocktail shaker. Add a few scoops of crushed ice, according to taste. Shake to blend well and thoroughly chill the mixture.

Strain into the prepared chocolate-rimmed glass. Serve, garnished with a peppermint stick or a fresh mint sprig.

Golden Sun Pumpkin Pie

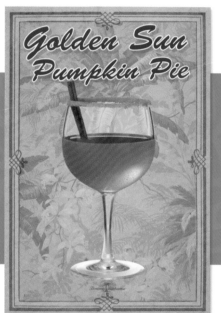

INGREDIENTS

1 tablespoon fine graham cracker crumbs

1½oz Tommy Bahama Golden Sun® rum

1oz pumpkin spice syrup

splash of whipping cream

Spread the graham cracker crumbs on a small plate. Wet the rim of a chilled glass, then dip it into the cracker crumbs to coat the rim well.

Place the rum, pumpkin spice syrup, and splash of whipping cream in a chilled cocktail shaker. Add a scoop or two of crushed ice, according to taste.

Shake until the mixture is well blended and thoroughly chilled. Strain into the prepared crumb-rimmed glass. Serve, garnished with a stick of cinnamon.

Nutty Sun

INGREDIENTS

1 tablespoon fine graham cracker crumbs

2oz Tommy Bahama Golden Sun® rum

1oz hazelnut liqueur

powdered cinnamon

Sprinkle the graham cracker crumbs over a small plate. Wet the rim of a chilled low glass, then dip it into the cracker crumbs to coat the rim well.

Pour the rum and hazelnut liqueur into a chilled cocktail shaker. Top off with a few scoops of crushed ice.

Shake until the mixture is thoroughly chilled and well blended. Pour into the prepared crumb-rimmed glass and sprinkle a little powdered cinnamon over the top. Serve, garnished with a cinnamon stick.

Golden Apple

INGREDIENTS

1oz Tommy Bahama Golden Sun® rum

2oz hot apple cider

Pour the rum and hot apple cider into a glass mug of your choice.

Stir to mix. Serve, garnished with a slice of fresh apple on the rim of the mug.

INGREDIENTS

2oz Tommy Bahama White Sand® rum

1 teaspoon superfine sugar

freshly squeezed juice of 1 lime

handful of fresh mint leaves, roughly chopped

club soda

Millionnaire Mojito

Place the rum, sugar, lime juice, and chopped mint leaves in a chilled cocktail shaker. Add some crushed ice, according to taste.

Shake until the mixture is well blended and chilled through.

Pour into a tall chilled glass. Top off with club soda.

Serve, garnished with a sprig of fresh mint and a slice of fresh lime.

Cosmopolitan

INGREDIENTS

1½oz Tommy Bahama White Sand® rum

⅓oz orange liqueur

⅓oz cranberry juice

⅓oz freshly squeezed lime juice

dash of simple (sugar) syrup

Place all the ingredients in a chilled cocktail shaker. Add a scoop or two of crushed ice, according to taste.

Shake well, until the mixture is thoroughly blended and icy cold.

Strain into a chilled martini glass. Serve, garnished with a twist of lime peel.

INGREDIENTS
Tommy Bahama White Sand® rum
crushed ice

Tommy-Tini

Measure out enough rum to almost fill a martini glass and pour into a chilled cocktail shaker. Add one or two scoops of crushed ice, according to taste.

Shake vigorously until the rum is well chilled and some of the ice has melted.

Strain into a chilled martini glass. Serve, garnished with a twist of fresh lime peel.

Tommy Bahama Bay Breeze

INGREDIENTS

2oz Tommy Bahama White Sand® rum

1oz pineapple juice

splash of cranberry juice

Pour all the ingredients into a chilled cocktail shaker. Add a large scoop of crushed ice. Shake until well mixed and thoroughly chilled through.

Half fill a low glass with fresh ice. Pour in the chilled cocktail mixture.

Serve, garnished with a wedge of fresh pineapple.

White Sand Cuba Libre

INGREDIENTS

1¾oz Tommy Bahama White Sand® rum

freshly squeezed juice of 1 lime

cola

Pour the rum and lime juice into a chilled highball glass that is about two-thirds filled with ice. Stir lightly to mix.

Top off with cola until the glass is full. Serve, garnished with a slice of fresh lime.

Bahama Sunrise

INGREDIENTS

1oz Tommy Bahama White Sand® rum
1oz grapefruit juice
1oz pineapple juice
club soda
grenadine syrup

Pour the rum, grapefruit juice, and pineapple juice into a chilled cocktail shaker. Add a scoop or two of crushed ice, according to taste.

Shake until the mixture is well blended and chilled through.

Tip into a chilled highball glass, add some fresh ice, then fill the glass with club soda. Stir briefly, top with a splash of grenadine and serve.

INGREDIENTS

1 tablespoon superfine sugar
1½oz Tommy Bahama White Sand® rum
1oz orange liqueur
1½oz freshly squeezed lime juice

Spread out the sugar on a small plate. Wet the rim of a chilled martini glass, then dip it into the sugar until the rim of the glass is well coated.

Pour the rum, orange liqueur, and lime juice into a chilled cocktail shaker. Add a couple of scoops of crushed ice, according to taste.

Shake vigorously until the mixture is well blended and chilled through.

Strain into the prepared sugar-rimmed martini glass. Serve, garnished with a slice of fresh lime.

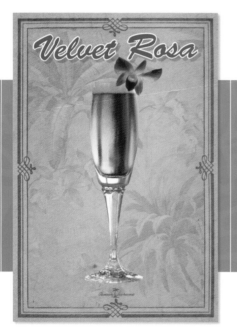

Velvet Rosa

INGREDIENTS

⅔oz Tommy Bahama White Sand® rum

⅓oz peach schnapps

1oz cranberry juice

Champagne

Put all the ingredients, except the Champagne, in a chilled cocktail shaker. Add a couple of scoops of crushed ice, according to taste.

Shake until well blended and the mixture is thoroughly chilled through.

Strain into a chilled champagne flute. Fill the glass with Champagne.

Stir briefly to bring out the effervescence. Serve, garnished with a small flower or a rose petal.

INGREDIENTS

2oz Baileys® Original Irish Cream

2oz Emmets® Classic Cream

1oz Coco Lopez® cream of coconut

½ fresh banana, peeled and roughly chopped

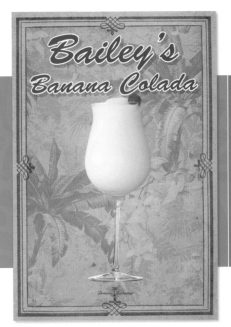

Bailey's Banana Colada

Place all the ingredients in the chilled goblet of a blender. Add a large scoop of crushed ice. Process until smooth.

Pour into a chilled hurricane glass. Serve, garnished with whipped cream and a maraschino cherry.

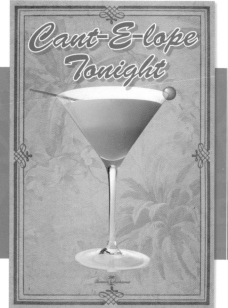

Cant-E-lope Tonight

INGREDIENTS

2oz watermelon liqueur

1oz premium vodka

1oz freshly squeezed orange·juice

½oz sour mix

Pour all the ingredients into a chilled cocktail shaker. Add a couple of scoops of crushed ice, according to taste.

Shake well until the mixture is thoroughly blended and ice cold.

Strain into a chilled martini glass. Serve garnished with a maraschino cherry on the rim.

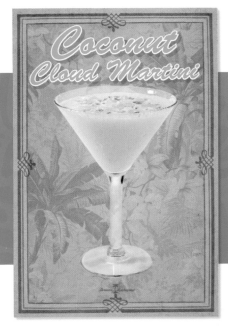

Coconut Cloud Martini

INGREDIENTS

1oz Tommy Bahama White Sand® rum

1½oz vanilla vodka

1½oz coconut liqueur

1oz cream of coconut

toasted coconut *(see page 153)*

Place all the ingredients in a chilled cocktail shaker. Add a few scoops of crushed ice, according to taste.

Shake vigorously until the mixture is thoroughly blended and well chilled.

Strain into a chilled martini glass. Top with a fine sprinkling of toasted coconut and serve.

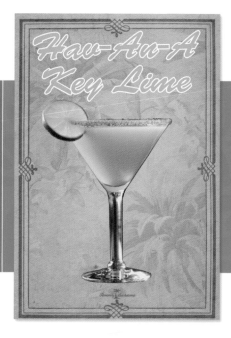

Hav-Au-A Key Lime

INGREDIENTS

1 tablespoon fine graham cracker crumbs

2oz vanilla vodka

2oz key lime cream liqueur

½oz freshly squeezed lime juice

Spread the graham cracker crumbs over a small plate. Wet the rim of a chilled cocktail glass and dip it into the cracker crumbs to coat the rim.

Place all the remaining ingredients in a chilled cocktail shaker. Add a scoop or two of crushed ice, according to taste.

Shake vigorously until the mixture is well blended and chilled.

Strain into the prepared crumb-rimmed glass. Serve, garnished with a slice of fresh lime.

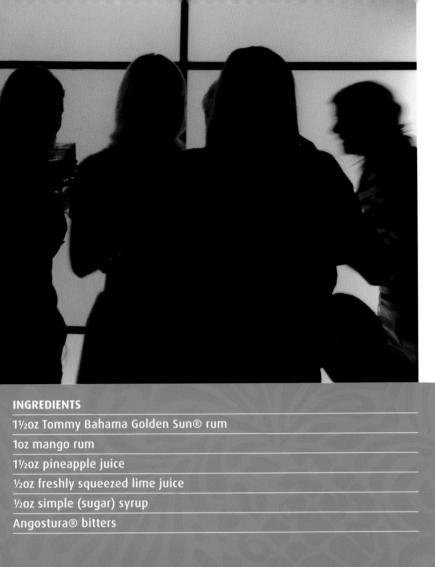

INGREDIENTS

1½oz Tommy Bahama Golden Sun® rum

1oz mango rum

1½oz pineapple juice

½oz freshly squeezed lime juice

½oz simple (sugar) syrup

Angostura® bitters

Bronx Bomber

Pour the rum, mango rum, pineapple juice, lime juice, and simple syrup into a chilled cocktail shaker. Add a dash or two of Angostura bitters, plus a few scoops of crushed ice, according to taste.

Shake vigorously until the mixture is well blended and chilled through.

Strain into a chilled tumbler and serve, garnished with a twist of lemon peel.

TOMMY BAHAMA® DIRECTORY

STORES

Alabama
Birmingham
The Summit Mall
205.967.8389

Arizona
Phoenix
Biltmore Fashion Park
602.508.9888

Scottsdale
Kierland Commons
480.607.3388

Tucson
La Encantada Mall
520.299.8830

California
Anaheim
Anaheim Garden Walk
714.829.1350

Carmel
Carmel Plaza
831.620.0302

Irvine
Irvine Spectrum
949.753.8808

La Jolla
Wall Street
858.551.8686

Los Angeles
The Grove
323.930.2888

Manhattan Beach
Manhattan Village
310.697.2688

Mission Viejo
The Shops at Mission Viejo
949.257.0268

Newport Beach
Corona del Mar Plaza
949.760.1886

Palm Desert
The Gardens on El Paseo
760.836.0288

Palo Alto
Stanford Shopping Center
650.566.8668

Pasadena
Paseo Colorado Mall
626.584.7888

San Diego
Fashion Valley
619.243.8868

San Francisco
San Francisco Centre
415.593.8800

San Jose
Santana Row
408.984.8688

Thousand Oaks
The Lakes
805.381.5486

Walnut Creek
Mt. Diablo
925.956.0886

Colorado
Denver
Cherry Creek Mall
720.207.2688

Connecticut
Uncasville
Mohegan Sun
860.886.8688

Florida
Boca Raton
Mizner Park
561.394.9060

Bonita Springs
Coconut Point
239.947.2203

Coral Gables
The Village of
Merrick Park
305.445.8896

Ft. Lauderdale
Las Olas Blvd.
954.527.8868

Relax Store
Las Olas Blvd.
954.343.9986

Jacksonville
St. Johns Town Center
904.620.8868

Naples
3rd Street
239.643 .7920

RELAX Store
3rd Street South
239.213.1683

Orlando
Mall at Millenia
407.248.8286

Pointe Orlando
321.281.5886

Palm Beach Gardens
The Gardens Mall
561.909.1886

Sandestin
Grand Boulevard
850.650.0731

Sarasota
St. Armand's Circle
941.388.2446

Tampa
International Plaza
813.319.8860

Old Hyde Park Village
813.258.8688

Wellington
The Mall at Wellington
Green
561.792.2868

West Palm Beach
City Place
561.491.6688

Georgia
Atlanta
Phipps Plaza
404.591.8868

Hawaii
Honolulu
Ala Moana Center
808.955.8869

Ka'anapali
Whaler's Village
808.661.8823

Kohala Coast
The Shops at Mauna Lani
808.881.8688

Waikoloa
Kings' Shops
808.886.8865

Wailea
The Shops at Wailea
808.879.7828

Illinois
Chicago
Michigan Avenue
312.644.8388

Northbrook
Northbrook Court
847.656.0860

Indiana
Indianapolis
The Fashion Mall
at Keystone
317.569.0866

Massachusetts
Boston
Natick Collection
508.655.8855

Michigan
Troy
Somerset Collection
South
248.283.1886

Minnesota
Bloomington
Mall of America
952.351.9888

Missouri
Kansas City
The Country Club Plaza
816.531.8688

Nevada
Las Vegas
Fashion Show Mall
702.731.6868

Forum Shops at Caesars
702.933.6888

Miracle Mile Shops
702.731.3988

Town Square Las Vegas
702.948.6828

RESTAURANTS & BARS

New Jersey
Atlantic City
The Pier Shops at Caesars
609.348.5268

North Carolina
Charlotte
Southpark Mall
704.364.0686

Oregon
Tigard
Bridgeport Village
971.327.7488

South Carolina
Charleston
Shops at Charleston Place
843.723.0668

Myrtle Beach
The Market Common
843.839.0880

Texas
Austin
The Domain
512.852.5001

Dallas
Dallas Galleria
214.540.8628

West Village
214.219.8688

San Antonio
La Cantera
210.587.3660

The Woodlands
Market Street
281.292.6878

Virginia
McLean
Tyson's Galleria
703.564.2688

Richmond
Short Pump Town Center
804.364.8862

Washington
Seattle
University Village
206.826.8030

Arizona
Scottsdale
Kierland Commons
480.505.3668

California
Newport Beach
The Island Grille at
Corona del Mar Plaza
949.760.8686

Palm Desert
The Gardens on El Paseo
760.836.0188

Florida
Naples
3rd Street
239.643.6889

Orlando
Pointe Orlando
321.281.5888

Sandestin
Grand Boulevard
850.654.1743

Sarasota
St. Armand's Circle
941.388.2888

Hawaii
Kohala Coast
The Shops at Mauna Lani
808.881.8686

Wailea
The Shops at Wailea
808.875.9983

Nevada
Las Vegas
Town Square Las Vegas
702.948.8006

South Carolina
Myrtle Beach
The Market Common
843.839.1868

Texas
The Woodlands
Market Street
281.292.8669

INTERNATIONAL STORES

Australia
Queensland
Main Beach
Marina Mirage
74 Seaworld Drive
61.7.55313088

Noosa Heads
Netanya
75 Hastings Street
61.7.54472328

Port Douglas
Club Tropical
Macrossan & Wharf Street
61.7.40996699

Canada
British Columbia
Vancouver
Oakridge Shopping Center
650 West 41st Avenue,
Unit 187
604.261.8283

West Vancouver
Village at Royal Park
825 Main Street, Unit G4
604.925.3000

Ontario
Oakville
216 Lakeshore Road East
905.849.4190

Port Carling (Seasonal)
Muskoka
123 Medora Street, Unit 1
705.765.0767

Willowdale
Bayview Village
2901 Bayview Ave., Unit 29
416.223.3919

United Arab Emirates
Dubai
Ocean Bliss—Royal Mirage
Hotel
Jumeirah Beach Road
9.714.315.2177

Mall of the Emirates
Sheikh Zayed Road
9.714.341.0791

Souk Madinat Jumeirah
Jumeirah
9.714.368.6031

FUTURE STORES
For up-to-the-minute information, check the
Store Locator on our website regularly or sign up
for email alerts to be the first to hear about new
store and restaurant openings.

www.tommybahama.com

ACKNOWLEDGMENTS

The publisher would like to thank the following for their kind permission to reproduce their photographs:

(Key: a-above; b-below/bottom; c-center; f-far; l-left; r-right; t-top)

Alamy Images: Brownstock Inc. 57fbl; Andre Jenny 57cra; Life File Photo Library Ltd 159cl; Picture Contact 158-159; **Corbis:** Peter Adams 88cra; Atlantide Phototravel 84crb, 90br, 127bl; Craig Aurness 42, 136-137; Jim Barber 88tl; Paul Barton 193t; Benelux 142cra; Richard Broadwell/Beateworks 86b, 91; André Burian 178t; Olivier Cadeaux 55cl; Angelo Cavalli 113, 129cra; Michael Clark/Aurora Photos 30-31; Ralph A. Clevenger 55 (fish); Comstock Select 57br; Ashley Cooper 39br; Corbis Yellow 134cra; Creasource 59br; Cross Wave/amanaimages 37clb; Jim Cummins 53b; Larry Dale Gordon 14-15; Joshua Dalsimer 57tl; Fridmar Damm 47b; Sean Davey/Australian Picture Library 54, 171tr; Dex 145cra; George B. Diebold 165tl; DiMaggio/Kalish 198-199b; Emely 37tr; Macduff Everton 84tl, 132t; Fadil 139b; Jon Feingersh/Blend Images 41tc; Flayols/SoFood 47tl; Flirt 151t, 200-201; Patrick Fraser 88clb; Jose Fuste Raga 133t; Carson Ganci/Design Pics 168b; Bertrand Gardel/Hemis 106clb; Goodshoot 153t; Rob Gracie 55bl; Darren Greenwood/Design Pics 57bl, 57tr; George Hammerstein 57 (background); Rolf W. Hapke 161tr; Noel Hendrickson 55tl; Dana Hoff/Beateworks 40; Jason Hosking 147cra; Image Source 114clb; image100 132bl; Hola Images 109; ImageShop 41cb; K. Imamura 104b; Inspirestock 160b; Mark A. Johnson 55cr; Joson 121, 169b; Juice Images 161b; Reed Kaestner 163tl; Ronnie Kaufman 37t; Herbert Kehrer 36; Frank Krahmer 11t, 43 (waterfall), 106tl; Bob Krist 5; Bob Krist/amanaimages 192tr; Frans Lanting 190tl; Randy Lincks 119; Maoi Lopez/epa 157 (background); Simon Marcus 12cl; Grafton Marshall Smith 59c; Mascarucci 72b; Joe McBride 172-173; MedioImages 160tl, 190tr; Moodboard 41cr, 56; Laurence Mouton/PhotoAlto 118cla; Muriot/PhotoCuisine 13br; Mitsushi Okada/amanaimages 2-3, 60-61; Sakis Papadopoulos 143br; Douglas Peebles 103; PhotoCuisine 45tl, 47clb, 144t; Javier Pierini 162t; Mike Powell 57cr; Radius 140b; Radius Images 160tr; Redlink 59 (background); G. P. Reichelt 168tr; Olivier Renck/Aurora Photos 39c; Pete Saloutos 180tl; Richard Schultz 59tc; Hugh Sitton 43tr; Sprint 13tr; Joerg Steffens 55cb; David Stoecklein 162b; Subiros/PhotoCuisine 41cl; Surf 148t; Steve Terrill 73; Klaus Tiedge 146b; TongRo 149b; Elke van de Velde 108b; Onne van der Wal 58, 59bl, 59tr, 108clb; Karl Weatherly 55tr; Michele Westmorland 72t; Stuart Westmorland 102b; Ed Young/AgStock Images 124tc; **Dorling Kindersley:** Stephen Oliver 39tr; **Getty Images:** AAGAMIA 179b; Steve Allen 13c, 175tl; altrendo nature 178b, 181tr; Charlie Baird 165b; Joao Canziani 186b; Julien Capmeil 38; Steve Casimiro 167tr; Angelo Cavalli 43tl, 176tl, 194tl; Christopher Seufert Photography 171b; Kathy Collins 166t; Diane Cook and Len Jenshel 196tr; Livia Corona 195b; Mark Cosslett 43clb; Thomas Cristofoletti 182tl; Creative Crop 53tl; Ian Cumming 189b; Richard Cummins 188tr; Todd Davidson 161tl; Peter Dazeley 158clb; De Agostini Picture Library 195tl; Michael DeFreitas 190b; Digital Vision 11br; Dorgie Productions 187tl; Dosfotos 49tl; Neil Emmerson 166b; Britt Erlanson 44; Macduff Everton 191tr; Grant Faint 191b; Foodcollection 105; Robert Francis 167b; Stephen Frink 12cr; Glowimages 52, 194b; Stuart Gregory 46; Peter Gridley 197b; Jamie Grill 47ftl; Michael Grimm 12cla; Darrell Gulin 182-183, 197tr; Martin Harvey 13bl, 41tr; Tom Haseltine 169tl; Robert Holland 187b; Andrew Holt 164t; Kerrick James Photography 192b; Lynn James 188b; Jupiterimages 196b; Jonathan Kantor 196cl; John Kelly 186t; Anthony Lanneretonne 102c; George Lepp 197tl; Holger Leue 129b; Wayne Levin 170b; Mark Lewis 49cla, 191tl, 192tl; Sean Locke 53tc; Ludovic Maisant 12bc, 167tl; Hiroyuki Matsumoto 49cra; Aaron McCoy 176tr; Ian Murray 80ca; Donald Nausbaum 163tr; Amy Neunsinger 72cl; Clive Nichols 194tr; Pete Orelup 170tl; Frederic Pacorel 179tr; Panoramic Images 49clb, 187tr; Plush Studios 174t; Ingrid Rasmussen 48; Darren Robb 196tl; Lisa Romerein 47 (salads); Rose/Myller 53crb; Jonathan Savoie 170-171; Kevin Schafer 183b; Preston Schlebusch 174b; Jochen Schlenker 180-181; Paul Souders 71; Otto Stadler 179tl; Stockbyte 43r; Paul Sutherland 104tl; Mark R. Thomas 198-199t; Tohoku Color Agency 49 (background); Darryl Torckler 55br; Raul Touzon 163b; Mike Truelove 177t; Robert Van Der Hilst 164b; Annika Vannerus 49bl; Peeter Viisimaa 189tr; Caroline von Tuempling 45c; Dougal Waters 49br, 195tr; Anne-Marie Weber 176b; Ingmar Wesemann 185tr; Michele Westmorland 177b; Andy Whale 53cra; Jeremy Woodhouse 175b; **iStockphoto.com:** aldra 37br; Lena Andersson 131t; Christopher Badzioch 147cl; Claudio Baldini 124cl; Poppy Barach 76tl; Galina Barskaya 45br; BasSlabbers 35cr; Don Bayley 144br; Andreas Belias 78ca; Chris Bence 68cl; Barbro Bergfeldt 143tl; Kelly Cline 45cl; James Colin 98b; creacart 98cra, 138b; Shane Cummins 80clb; Royce DeGrie 156; Sabrina dei Nobili 59cla; Le Do 66br; DurdenImages 45cr; Artem Efimov 150b; eyewave 127br, 140cra; Carlos Fierro 34-35t; Viktor Fischer 120bl, 120tl, 150t, 151b; FotografiaBasica 124cra; fotoIE 45tr (white); fotolinchen 144cra; David Freund 45bl; Jill Fromer 131bl; Jean Gill 68b; Mark Gillow 128t; Richard Gunion 70tl; Ermin Gutenberger 78br, 116ca; Andrew Hyslop 126t; ilbusca 98cl; Gabor Izso 45tr (pink), 138crb; janeff 87; Kristen Johansen 70cla; Denise Jones 78tl; Charlotte Karlbom 39bl; Sebastian Kaulitzki 41tl; kemie 11br (photo edge), 11tr (photo edge), 34 (photo edge), 42 (photo edge), 52 (photo edge), 54 (photo edge); Melanie Kintz 86tl; Ivan Kmit 96br; Aleksandar Kolundzija 130tc; Zbigniew Kościelniak 153b; Yelena Kovalenko 43cr; Ruslan Kudrin 39crb; Alberto L. Pomares G. 43ca; Rudi Lange 43cla; Kate Leigh 43cra; Scott Leigh 84bl; Robert Lerich 131br; Mark Lijesen 135tr; loupblanc 78bl; Viktor Lugovskoy 74tl; Olga Lyubkina 104cl; Maceofoto 147t; Robyn Mackenzie 96bl; Antonis Magnissalis 127tl; William Mahar 76ca, 129t; Anna Marinova 145b; Miranda McMurray 126br; James McQuillan 64clb, 148b; Vladimir Melnik 99; Juan Monino 66cla, 74cl; NWphotoguy 86cra; Matt Olsen 39cl; pederk 147b; Luis Pedrosa 140t; George Peters 151cra; Uros Petrovic 141b; Ben Phillips 152t; PLAINVIEW 134cl; Noel Powell 98tl; Jack Puccio 96tl, 130cra; Steve Rabin 139t; Tina Rencelj 125t; Amanda Rohde 5 (photo edge); Frans Rombout 94cra; Matthew Scherf 134b; Angelika Schwarz 45 (background); Suzannah Skelton 70bl, 102tl; David Smith 138t; Kathleen & Scott Snowden 45fbr; Snowshill 39t; SoleilC 112ca; Alina Solovyova-Vincent 133bl; Rob Stegmann 96cla, 134tl; Klaudia Steiner 64br; subjug 47 (tablecloth); thepropshoppe 74ca; Stefanie Timmermann 126cl; Tootles 153cra; Paul Turner 112clb; Marek Uliasz 145t; Annett Vauteck 142b; Sebastian Vera 104cra, 132crb; Joan Vicent Cantó 128br; Cindy Xiao 76br; YinYang 106b; ziggymaj 97; zolwiks 141t.

All other images © Tommy Bahama